Physical Characteristics of the Sussex Spaniel

(from the American Kennel Club breed standard)

Body: Low and long with a level topline.

Tail: Docked from 5 to 7 inches and set low.

Hindquarters: Full and well-rounded, strong and heavily boned. They should be parallel with each other and also set wide apart. The hind legs are short from the hock to the ground, heavily boned. The hindquarters must correspond in angulation to the forequarters.

Color: Rich golden liver is the only acceptable color.

Height: Measured at the withers ranges from 13 to 15 inches.

Weight: Ranges between 35 and 45 pounds.

short hair between the toes.

D1566332

Sussex Spaniel

By Becki Jo Hirschy

Contents

3 9082 10774 1368

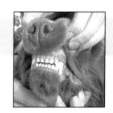

KENNEL CLUB BOOKS® SUSSEX SPANIEL
ISBN: 1-59378-359-0

Copyright © 2007 • Kennel Club Books, LLC • 308 Main Street, Allenhurst, NJ 07711 USA
Cover Design Patented: US 6,435,559 B2 • Printed in South Korea

Library of Congress Cataloging-in-Publication Data
Hirschy, Becki Jo.
  Sussex spaniel / by Becki Jo Hirschy.
    p. cm.
  ISBN 1-59378-359-0
  1. Sussex spaniel. I. Title.
  SF429.S88H57 2006
  636.752'4—dc22
                                     2006012320
          10 9 8 7 6 5 4 3 2 1

Photography by Carol Ann Johnson
with additional photographs by:

Ashbey Photography, Norvia Behling, Booth Photography by Monica, Paulette Braun, Carolina Biological Supply, Isabelle Français, Bill Jonas, Don and Becky Krueger, Dr. Dennis Kunkel, Tam C. Nguyen, Phototake, Jean Claude Revy, Dr. Andrew Spielman, Chuck Tatham, Alice van Kempen and Otto Wahl.

Illustrations by Patricia Peters.

The publisher wishes to thank all of the owners whose dogs are featured in this book, including Jean Burnett, Beth Dowd, Jeane Haverick, Jan Hepper, Don and Becky Krueger, Helen Marshall, Erin Miller, Lindsey Miller, Dr. Marlin and Sheila Reaknow, Cecelia Ruggles, Linda Shannon and Liz Shewell.

The Sussex Spaniel is one of the most rare of the sporting spaniels. It originated in southeastern England in the late 1700s and has evolved through the centuries. Today the breed is known equally for its pet and show qualities as well as hunting ability.

SUSSEX SPANIEL

One of the oldest types of dog, the "Spanyell" was mentioned in literature as early as 1386 and portraits of spaniel-type dogs adorn many Old Master paintings. Although the term "spaniel" has been used widely as a descriptive term from the 17th century on, since the latter 19th century the spaniels primarily have been considered as English dogs, and so it is with the Sussex Spaniel.

One of the rarest of the sporting spaniels, the Sussex Spaniel originated in southeastern England. Breeding dogs of no particular lineage, denoted in kennel records as "Bebb to Fan" or "Old Bebb to Flirt," resulted in the appearance of the Sussex Spaniel as a more-or-less distinct spaniel type. While it is possible to trace the Sussex Spaniel back well into the late 1700s, credit is given to Mr. Augustus Elliot Fuller (Rosehill kennels) as the founder of the breed. He kept Sussex Spaniels as working dogs on his estate through the mid-1800s.

The Sussex County region gave the breed its name and had

Circa 1620, this scene from *The Vision of St. Hubert* depicts different types of hound- and spaniel-like dogs, some of which are likely the predecessors of today's gundog breeds. The original painting is housed in the Prado Museum, Madrid.

much to do with the original vision of the breed as a strong and untiring spaniel, fully capable of negotiating the heavy clay soil of the region, which supported thick and somewhat daunting cover. Shorter legs, ability to maneuver, a massive body and innate desire rendered the breed ideally suited for hunting this habitat.

Interestingly, this heavy clay soil has a distinctly golden tinge to its coloration, not at all unlike the golden liver color that is truly a hallmark of the Sussex Spaniel. Perhaps this blending of the dogs with their surroundings resulted

in a preference for dogs that used their voices when hunting. After all, when a dog blends into cover, the dog's voice surely alerts the

LIVER TO LIVER

In 1872, a rule was enacted that only Sussex of the liver coat color, who were out of two dogs similarly liver in coat color, were allowed to be shown. This may well have been an effort of sorts at "purity" since, despite the lack of modern DNA testing, it was known at that time that breeding liver to liver only begets liver-colored animals.

hunter to the location of his dog! Although contested by many modern fanciers, historically the Sussex Spaniel is the sole spaniel said to "give tongue"—a rather distinctive sound—when on the hunt.

Though Mr. Fuller is often purported to be the "father" of the Sussex Spaniel as a breed, according to many accounts, it is likely more factual to say that Mr. Fuller simply kept and bred his own strain of spaniel for the purpose of shooting over in the Sussex region. Mr. Fuller did, however, do much to develop the unique golden liver color in his Rosehill strain, with the assis-

tance of his kennel manager, Albert Reif.

With the evolution of the dog show, and later of written standards of perfection for individual breeds, then, as now, fanciers concentrated on producing winners. A rare breed like the Sussex Spaniel was surely attractive for early dog show exhibitors, with its handsome features and solid working ability. After all, in the early days of the dog show, functional abilities were important.

Early fanciers of the Sussex Spaniel in that era were also fanciers of other spaniel breeds. The first Stud Book of The Kennel Club in England shows

In the early 20th century, Mrs. Youell was considered one of the most important breeders of the Sussex Spaniel. Her kennel prefix, Earlswood, stood for top quality in the breed.

INTERBRED REGISTRY

Until 1931 in the UK, offspring of two varieties of spaniel mated together could be registered and subsequently shown as either variety. After 1931, the interbred spaniel registry came into existence. Thereafter, offspring of the matings of two varieties of spaniel were required to be registered as interbred.

that Field, English Cocker and Sussex Spaniels were lumped together under one heading. Interbreeding of the three spaniel types was more the rule than the exception, with offspring shown as the variety that they most resembled.

Mr. Phineas Bullock is one such fancier and a lead character in the revival of the breed that took place in the 1870s. One of his main studs was a dog named Bebb. Mr. Bullock sold this dog, reportedly later regretting that moment of weakness, as Bebb became quite influential in the Sussex Spaniel's development. As merely one illustration of the vast amount of interbreeding between the various spaniel varieties, Bebb's name appears as an ancestor in the extension of the pedigrees of every Sussex, Field and English Cocker Spaniel in the world today.

Though entered in the Stud Book as a Sussex Spaniel of liver color, written critiques of Bebb indicate that his chief Sussex feature was his coat color, since descriptions of his features were quite different from those ascribed to the Sussex Spaniel. Again, this merely exemplifies the

Lovely specimens of their time, Sussex Spaniels Eng. Ch. Rosehill Rock and Eng. Ch. Rosehill Rag were bred and owned by Campbell Newington, Esq., of Oakover, Ticehurst, Sussex, England, and portrayed beautifully in this painting by Lilian Cheviot.

notion of "spaniel soup" in the late 1800s. The relative "purity" of bloodlines was not as closely protected at that time as in the modern era.

Throughout the late 1800s, the Sussex Spaniel remained rare and numbers were low. Mr. Moses Woolland (Bridford kennels) and Mr. Campbell Newington (Rosehill, revived) took a fancy to the Sussex Spaniel. Their kennels established breeding programs that had far-reaching effects, though probably also contributed further to diminished numbers in the breed. These two kennels monopolized the breed in such a way that it likely had a discouraging effect on others who would endeavor to fancy the breed.

In fits and starts, the Sussex Spaniel tenaciously survived through the end of World War I, with fanciers coming and going in the breed. At that time, Mr. Stevenson Clarke (Broadhurst kennels) took a keen interest in the Sussex for its working qualities, while also having a moderate interest in dog shows. The Broadhurst line contained significant Field Spaniel blood, and it is no surprise that these dogs were correspondingly longer in leg and foreface than the ideal. By 1924, there was sufficient interest to form the Sussex Spaniel Association (England) for the "protection of the Sussex Spaniel."

Between the World Wars, other fanciers took up the breed, notably several women: Miss Reed (Oakerland kennels), Miss Wigg (Hornshill kennels) and Mrs. Joy Freer (nee Scholefield) of the famed Fourclovers Sussex Spaniel kennels. Photos of the dogs from these kennels show more typical Sussex Spaniel outlines and overall type. Yet, only the Fourclovers kennel kept the breed going during the years

The Field Spaniel's ancestry is closely interwoven with that of the Sussex.

A documented crossbreeding to a Clumber Spaniel was undertaken in an attempt to revive the Sussex breed in the years after World War II.

Today's Sussex Spaniel, looking ahead to a promising future.

of World War II, such that another revival of the breed became a necessity. Indeed, by the end of the war, there was a grand total of eight Sussex Spaniels remaining in England, all from Mrs. Freer's Fourclovers kennel. It is important to note that all modern Sussex Spaniels owe a debt of monumental proportions to Mrs. Freer. Without her interest, dedication and perseverance, which continued for some 60 years, it is unlikely that the breed would have survived.

The breed continued to emerge from near-extinction slowly through the 1950s, with years in which difficulty in breeding resulted in no new Sussex Spaniel puppies. In an effort to assist the breed's survival, one officially recorded interbreeding was undertaken with Thornville Snowstorm, a Clumber Spaniel. Three generations of this cross were absorbed into Sussex Spaniel lines. Other crossbreedings, such as that to the English Springer Spaniel, Brownie, can be documented through extrapolation. A Sussex Spaniel, Timothy of Oakerland, appears in the English Stud Book, having been sired by Sunny South, who, in turn, was out of Brownie, the Springer.

RECOGNITION

Sussex Spaniels were shown in England as early as 1862. This characteristically golden liver dog was also among the first ten breeds recognized by the American Kennel Club in 1894.

It is important to note these crosses. With the need to inbreed due to the small number of Sussex Spaniels available for breeding, each generation concentrates not only the Sussex Spaniel genes but also those of its ancestors. These documented crosses, along with the "spaniel soup" from the earliest development of the breed, likely account for the wide variation of type seen, particularly through the 1950s and 1960s, when long legs and untypical heads frequently were produced.

The breed became more settled in type, though still having variation, through the 1970s and 1980s, when a small group of people dedicated to the Sussex Spaniel concentrated on bringing the good specimens forward. Numbers have crept upward slowly such that today the Sussex Spaniel enjoys perhaps the most solid foothold on survival ever.

The Sussex Spaniel was among the first breeds to be recognized by the American Kennel Club (AKC), even though there were virtually no Sussex Spaniels in the US. While there were a few Sussex recorded by the AKC through the early 1900s, the registration of the UK import Oak Mermaid in 1924 marked the beginning of an American line that lasted through several generations.

Slowly but surely more American fanciers found the Sussex Spaniel an ideal breed into which to pour their efforts so that by the end of World War II, there were more Sussex Spaniels in the US than in England! Sadly this early auspicious beginning was not to last, and no American-bred Sussex Spaniel today has any of the dogs of the 1940s in their extended pedigrees.

Between 1957 and 1972, there were no Sussex Spaniel litters born in the US. The Sussex Spaniel required someone to champion and promote the breed,

The Best of Breed Sussex Spaniel at England's prestigious Crufts Dog Show in 2000.

Ch. Three D Stonecroft Endeavor, handled by Doug Johnson, was a multiple Best in Show winner in 1998.

Best of Breed at Westminster in 2000 was Ch. Eadweard's Almond Joy. The judge was Dr. J. Donald Jones.

to step forward and put forth the effort to re-establish the Sussex in the US. In 1970, Ch. Oakmoss Witch CD was imported from England into the US by George and Marcia Deugan to become a foundation for their Ziyadeh kennel. The role of the Ziyadeh line in ensuring the survival of the breed in the US cannot be minimized. With the addition of the Wilred line, established by William and Margaret Reid, and the Lexxfield line, established by

John Robert Lewis, Jr., the Sussex Spaniel gained a firm presence in the US that continues today.

While he continues to be a rare-breed spaniel, the Sussex Spaniel has gained recognition in recent years in a variety of venues but particularly on the American dog-show scene. A remarkable "little brown dog" captured many hearts when he achieved a milestone for the breed: the first-ever Group One (first place in the Sporting Group) award at the nationally televised Westminster Kennel Club show in 2004. This dog, Ch. Clussexx Three D Grinchy Glee, known as "Stump," amassed an enviable show record and numerous Best in Show awards in addition to his Westminster Group win. In fact, Best in Show awards have been earned by no fewer than nine Sussex Spaniels in recent years! When this show-ring success is added to the breed's good-natured companionability, versatility in many performance endeavors and naturally good looks, one can see why the Sussex Spaniel enjoys a firm foothold in America today.

The all-time top winning Sussex Spaniel, Ch. Clussexx Three D Grinchy Glee ("Stump"), broke records as one of America's top show dogs of all breeds in 2004, winning 37 Bests in Show that year alone. He is shown winning at Wisconsin Rapids Kennel Club under judge Dr. Robert Berndt, handled by Scott Sommers.

CHARACTERISTICS OF THE

SUSSEX SPANIEL

PERSONALITY

A somber expression, emphasized by a furrowed brow that gives the impression of a somewhat sad frown, belies the calm and steady nature of the Sussex Spaniel. The breed has a distinct personality, and traits cherished by fanciers are the cheerful outlook on life and the extreme loyalty of the Sussex to hearth and home. Showing a distinct preference for his owners, the Sussex may be somewhat aloof, while at the same time polite and gentle, to strangers. Reserve upon first meetings is markedly different from shyness and should not be confused as such. The reserved Sussex will look over the stranger and, upon sensing his owners' acceptance of the new person, will accept the individual into his circle of friends as well.

Fond of communicating their emotions, the Sussex will use his expressive eyes to his advantage, often while vocalizing with a rather odd snort. It is not unusual for fanciers to refer to the breed as comical; indeed, many Sussex are comedians who develop a plethora of funny little antics that

as much amuse as exasperate their owners. In any gathering of Sussex fanciers, one is at once taken by the stories that abound of the activities of their dogs, who love to be the center of attention in the household. One comical trait that many Sussex show is a rather gopher-like position in which the dog sits up upon his haunches as if to beg. Another such trait is the tendency of some Sussex to "grin," where the dog draws back his lips to expose his teeth.

While a Sussex may be content at times to be a "couch potato," do not be fooled—this is a lively breed with plenty of energy to keep up with an active family. An affectionate dog, this powerful spaniel has a strong personality and will seek to be involved in every aspect of his owner's life.

This is a fine breed, and, in the words of Mrs. Freer, "...beware, if you become bitten by the Sussex bug, there is no known cure and good sense and reason can quickly go out the window. However, if you want a challenge and wish to work a fine

The somber, somewhat sad look is typical of the Sussex Spaniel's expression but contradicts the breed's happy personality.

traditional spaniel breed, then perhaps you should take a second look at the little brown jobs." It is common for many Sussex owners to describe themselves as being owned by their dogs; this says much about the personality of the breed and their affinity for human companionship.

A PICTURE OF THE SUSSEX SPANIEL

In the initial view, the Sussex Spaniel must be seen as the sum of his parts to properly appreciate the overall balance of the long, low, level and strong rectangular outline that is part and parcel of the breed. While the term "massive" is used in modern standards for the breed, the impression of overall size immediately must imply the breed's purpose: to conquer dense undergrowth *en route* to flushing game within gun range of the hunter, who is afoot. Too much mass in comparison to

the overall body size, reminiscent of the mass of the Clumber Spaniel, impedes the breed's stamina and ability to maneuver when afield. Too little mass, often seen with relatively longer, lighter-boned legs, implies a speed for work that leads to going around, rather than through, heavy cover.

The American Kennel Club specifies height as between 13 to 15 inches. Sufficient bone and muscling contribute to the overall mass such that the Sussex should weigh around 50 pounds; again, bitches are likely to weigh less than dogs and weight will be in proportion to height.

Following the initial impression of the outline of the Sussex Spaniel, one is drawn quickly to the handsome head, with its somber, serious expression. The impression when perusing the face of the Sussex is that of a frown that is never fierce or foreboding but rather contemplative and serious. While overall virtue of the animal should never rest solely on the qualities of the head, the head of the Sussex Spaniel contributes as much to the distinctive appearance of the breed as the overall proportion, balance, depth and bone of the body. To emphasize one attribute at the expense of another does the breed no service.

When viewed from the top, the skull is relatively wide yet

The distinct golden liver color, a true hallmark of the breed, is reminiscent of the clay soil of the region in which the Sussex was bred to work.

rectangular, maintaining a length sufficient to avoid equal proportions of length to width. Without this slightly rectangular shape, the head will appear heavy. Characteristic of the breed, the median furrow (center indentation) and heavy brow frame large eyes that are gentle, soft and languishing, as if to draw one into the very soul of the dog. The eyes are hazel, in keeping with the gilded liver color of the coat, and may show a slight amount of haw. Too much looseness to the eye is a liability to the working Sussex, as the dog will be prone to eye irritation at the least from dust, seeds and other irritants inherent in the field environment. With a pronounced stop (the area between mid-brow and muzzle), the face is framed by lobular, large ears, set slightly above the outer corner of the eye and lying close to the skull.

Beneath the eyes, the muzzle is broad and somewhat square when viewed in profile. Ideally somewhat shorter in length and never longer than the topskull, the muzzle is finished with a large nose that is liver in color, with wide-open nostrils. There is no upward or downward slope to the muzzle and the nasal bone is straight, thereby giving the optimal channel for scenting. The lips are somewhat pendulous. Moderation is the key here, as the dog must be able to pick up game cleanly without interference of the

Size difference in the Sussex is visible, as the bitch (LEFT) is generally shorter and smaller than the dog (RIGHT).

flews; it is not a desirable thing for the dog to bite his own lip when retrieving.

Beneath the lips, the bite is ideally a scissors bite, i.e., the upper teeth closely overlapping the lower teeth and set squarely to the jaws. While a scissors bite generally is accepted as being less injurious to game on the retrieve, the bite has less to do with bringing back a bird fit for consumption than does the quality of the mouth. In and of itself, the bite does not denote any tendency toward hard or soft mouth, and deviations from the perfect scissors bite simply are faults.

The head is set onto a well-arched and muscular neck that implies strength. Make no mistake—the proper neck is absolutely necessary to the corresponding proper carriage of the large, strong head, which is rarely held above the level of the back. The head should meet the neck smoothly, without a pointed occiput; any tendency toward a

The Sussex must have the desired soft mouth to bring back the game undamaged. This is Lucy, hunting companion of Becky Krueger, owned by Don and Becky Krueger.

peaked appearance is not typical. In profile, the neck is clean and without excessive skin.

When viewed from the side, the topline of the Sussex is level and firm with a deep, well-developed chest. It must be emphasized that proper length of rib contributes to the level topline; dogs without sufficient length of rib cage will not be able to hold a proper topline, as there is no supporting structure. The rib blends into a well-developed, short and strong loin that has no appearance of a waist.

The tail is typically docked so that it is 5 to 7 inches in length for a mature animal. The tail is merely an extension of the spine and, as such, is set and carried low. When gaiting, the tail has a lively action but never is carried above the level of the back.

Shoulders are set well back and the upper arm corresponds

in length to the shoulder blade so that the legs are able to move properly. Forelegs are short, straight and heavily boned, nicely clothed in feathering and set well under the body. Hindquarters must match the bone of the forequarters beneath a strong well rounded and muscular haunch. The rear hock is short and strong and turns neither in nor out when viewed from the rear. Both front and rear feet are large and round in appearance, with short hair between the toes. Good padding of the feet is absolutely necessary for an animal that works dense cover.

When on the move, the Sussex is lively and typically

WEBSITES FOR SUSSEX SPANIEL INFORMATION

www.sussexspaniels.org
The official AKC parent club of the Sussex Spaniel. Much useful information to help you decide if this is the right breed for you.

www.akc.org
American Kennel Club website, which includes the AKC's Sussex standard, a photograph and quick facts on the breed.

www.sussexspaniels.org.uk
The Sussex Spaniel Association (United Kingdom).

HEART-HEALTHY
In this modern age of ever-improving cardio-care, no doctor or scientist can dispute the advantages of owning a dog to lower a person's risk of heart disease. Studies have proven that petting a dog, walking a dog and grooming a dog all show positive results toward lowering your blood pressure. The simple routine of exercising your dog—going outside with the dog and walking, jogging or playing catch—is heart-healthy in and of itself. If you are normally less active than your physician thinks you should be, adopting a dog may be a smart option to improve your own quality of life as well as that of another creature.

"rolling" as a result of the relatively short legs coupled with a long and sturdy body. Action of the front and rear legs is coordinated and powerful to propel the dog forward. One should be able to imagine the dog's negotiating heavy cover with ease. As such, any paddling, high-stepping or other energy-wasting motions are not typical.

The body coat is abundant and may be either flat or with a slight wave. The neck has a well-marked frill, and furnishings appear on the ears, the back of the forelegs, the rear quarters and the tail, although feathering on the rear hocks is short. Coat and color are highly important. A rich golden liver is the only acceptable color. Any tendency toward a dark liver color or toward a coarse, thin or "hound-type" coat is undesirable. The American standard states that a small patch of white on the chest is a minor fault, though white on any other part of the body is a major deviation from the breed standard.

HEALTH CONSIDERATIONS
Fortunately, health problems known in the Sussex Spaniel breed are fewer in number in comparison to many other breeds, particularly in consideration of the narrow genetic base of the Sussex. General good health seems to be a trait with which the breed, overall, is fortunate to be endowed. However, to be forewarned is to be forearmed, so there are some concerns that appear often enough to warrant discussion with breeders. Reputable breeders test their dogs for health problems and do not include affected dogs or carriers in their breeding programs.

HIP DYSPLASIA
Hip dysplasia is an abnormal development of the ball-and-socket apparatus of the hip joint, which is typically progressive with the growth and develop-

Do You Know about Hip Dysplasia?

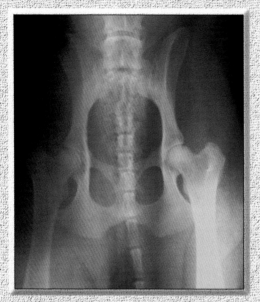

X-ray of a dog with "Good" hips.

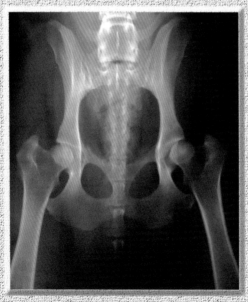

X-ray of a dog with "Moderate" dysplastic hips.

Hip dysplasia is a fairly common condition found in pure-bred dogs. When a dog has hip dysplasia, his hind leg has an incorrectly formed hip joint. By constant use of the hip joint, it becomes more and more loose, wears abnormally and may become arthritic.

Hip dysplasia can only be confirmed with an x-ray, but certain symptoms may indicate a problem. Your dog may have a hip dysplasia problem if he walks in a peculiar manner, hops instead of smoothly runs, uses his hind legs in unison (to keep the pressure off the weak joint), has trouble getting up from a prone position or always sits with both legs together on one side of his body.

As the dog matures, he may adapt well to life with a bad hip, but in a few years the arthritis develops and many dogs with hip dysplasia become crippled.

Hip dysplasia is considered an inherited disease and only can be diagnosed definitively by x-ray when the dog is two years old, although symptoms often appear earlier. Some experts claim that a special diet might help your puppy outgrow the bad hip, but the usual treatments are surgical. The removal of the pectineus muscle, the removal of the round part of the femur, reconstructing the pelvis and replacing the hip with an artificial one are all surgical interventions that are expensive, but they are usually very successful. Follow the advice of your veterinarian.

ment of the puppy to the adult dog. Symptoms have wide variation, from almost imperceptible to extreme pain and lameness. Virtually every country in which Sussex Spaniels reside has veterinary x-ray testing programs available to evaluate and grade the conformation of dogs' hip joints. While it is not a fail-safe prevention, as factors other than heredity come into play, research data worldwide conclude that breeding two parents that have tested normal for hip conformation tends to produce a higher percentage of puppies with healthy hips.

EYE ABNORMALITIES

Eye problems that can affect the Sussex Spaniel include entropion (eyelids that turn inward), ectropion (eyelids that turn somewhat outward to create a loose eye that shows haw) and cataracts. Many eye abnormalities are considered genetically transferred and testing programs are available. Again, breeding two parents that have tested free of eye disease tends to produce a higher percentage of puppies with healthy eyes.

HYPOTHYROIDISM

Low levels of thyroid hormones have been well known in the breed for a number of years and are thought by many veterinary researchers to contribute to other autoimmune disorders. While

Lower entropion, or rolling in of the eyelid, is causing irritation in the eye of this young dog. Several extra eyelashes, or distichiasis, are present on the lower lid.

there is some controversy over the heritable nature of the problem, it is safe to say that breeding two parents with normal thyroid function is likely to produce a higher percentage of puppies who will also have normal thyroid function. That being said, hypothyroidism is among the most treatable of any problem, involving annual blood testing and inexpensive daily medication.

CARDIAC ABNORMALITIES

Though puppies with cardiac defects often succumb at birth, some survive for a few years only to break the hearts of owners with early deaths. The most serious health concerns in the Sussex are cardiac in nature: patent ductus arteriosus (PDA), tetralogy of Fallot and pulmonic stenosis. It goes without saying that, before breeding, both parents should be cleared of cardiac defects by a vet with expertise in canine cardiology. Puppies should be examined for the presence of cardiac murmur prior to placement in homes.

SUSSEX SPANIEL

INTRODUCTION TO THE BREED STANDARD

In conformation showing, judges are looking for the dog that comes closest to the ideal described in the breed standard.

Breeders and fanciers share the common goal of producing Sussex Spaniels of correct type, handsome enough to win in the show ring yet imbued with innate ability and trainability to work in the field. Indeed, the ideal Sussex Spaniel is a versatile companion, well suited for many activities. It is important to remember the precarious and colorful history of the breed. All of the various dogs used to create the breed in the beginning, and the outcrosses to other spaniel breeds in the 1950s, will account for variation in type. One will see Sussex Spaniels who have a hint, and sometimes more, of these ancestors, evidenced by untypical appearance of the head and body. While there have been significant changes to the standard for the breed over the years, it is a severe injustice to the Sussex Spaniel for one to endeavor to breed, show or judge the Sussex without careful study and understanding of the breed standard.

THE AMERICAN KENNEL CLUB BREED STANDARD FOR THE SUSSEX SPANIEL

General Appearance: The Sussex Spaniel was among the first ten breeds to be recognized and admitted to the *Stud Book* when the American Kennel Club was formed in 1884, but it has existed as a

distinct breed for much longer. As its name implies, it derives its origin from the county of Sussex, England, and it was used there since the 18th century as a field dog. During the late 1800s the reputation of the Sussex Spaniel as an excellent hunting companion was well known among the estates surrounding Sussex County. Its short legs, massive build, long body and habit of giving tongue when on scent made the breed ideally suited to penetrating the dense undergrowth and flushing game within range of the gun. Strength, maneuverability and desire were essential for this purpose. Although it has never gained great popularity in numbers, the Sussex Spaniel continues today essentially unchanged in character and general appearance from those 19th century sporting dogs.

The Sussex Spaniel presents a long and low, rectangular and rather massive appearance coupled with free movements and nice tail action. The breed has a somber and serious expression. The rich golden liver color is unique to the breed.

Size, Proportion, Substance: *Size*—The height of the Sussex Spaniel as measured at the withers ranges from 13 to 15 inches. Any deviation from these measurements is a minor fault. The weight of the Sussex Spaniel

ranges between 35 and 45 pounds. *Proportion*—The Sussex Spaniel presents a rectangular outline as the breed is longer in body than it is tall. *Substance*—The Sussex Spaniel is muscular and rather massive.

Head: Correct head and expression are important features of the breed. *Eyes*—The eyes are hazel in color, fairly large, soft and languishing, but do not show the haw over-much. *Expression*—The Sussex Spaniel has a somber and serious appearance, and its fairly heavy brows produce a frowning expression. *Ears*—The ears are thick, fairly large and lobe-shaped and are set moderately low, slightly above the outside corner of the eye. *Skull and Muzzle*—The skull is moderately long and also wide with an indentation in the middle and with a full stop. The brows are

While the desirable soft mouth of a hunting spaniel has little to do with the actual bite, the correct bite in the Sussex should be a perfect scissors bite.

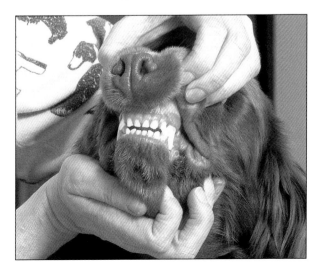

fairly heavy, the occiput is full but not pointed, the whole giving an appearance of heaviness without dullness. The muzzle should be approximately 3 inches long, broad and square in profile. The skull as measured from the stop to the occiput is longer than the muzzle. The nostrils are well-developed and liver colored. The lips are somewhat pendulous. *Bite*—A scissors bite is preferred. Any deviation from a scissors bite is a minor fault.

Neck, Topline, Body: *Neck*—The neck is rather short, strong and slightly arched, but does not carry the head much above the level of the back. There should not be much throatiness about the skin. *Topline and Body*—The whole body is characterized as low and long with a level topline. The chest is round, especially behind the shoulders, and is deep and wide which gives a good girth. The back and loin are long and very muscular both in width and depth. For this development, the back ribs must be deep. *Tail*—The tail is docked from 5 to 7 inches and set low. When gaiting the Sussex Spaniel exhibits nice tail action, but does not carry the tail above the level of the back.

Forequarters: The shoulders are well laid back and muscular. The upper arm should correspond in length and angle of return to the shoulder blade so that the legs are set well under the dog. The forelegs should be very short, strong and heavily boned. They may show a slight bow. Both straight and slightly bowed constructions are proper and correct. The pasterns are very short and heavily boned. The feet are large and round with short hair between the toes.

Hindquarters: The hindquarters are full and well-rounded, strong and heavily boned. They should be parallel with each other and also set wide apart—about as wide as the dog at the shoulders. The hind legs are short from the hock to the ground, heavily boned and should seem neither shorter than the forelegs nor much bent at the hocks. The hindquarters must correspond in angulation to the forequarters. The hocks should turn neither in nor out. The rear feet are like the front feet.

Coat: The body coat is abundant, flat or slightly waved, with no tendency to curl. The legs are moderately well-feathered, but clean below the hocks. The ears are furnished with soft, wavy hair. The neck has a well-marked frill in the coat. The tail is thickly covered with moderately long feather. No trimming is acceptable except to shape foot feather, or to remove feather between the pads or between the hock and the feet. The feather between the toes must be left in sufficient length to cover the nails.

FAULTS IN PROFILE

Ewe-necked; upright shoulders; dip in topline behind shoulders; arch over loin; weak, narrow front with toes out; narrow rear; cow-hocked; lacking angulation.

Too high on leg; lacking bone and substance; lacking angulation at both ends; high in rear; flat feet.

Short neck, poorly set onto upright shoulders; weak pasterns; flat feet; too heavy in shoulders, leading into soft topline; steep croup; tail set too low.

Short neck; loaded shoulders; high in rear; lacking proper angulation in rear.

Sussex Spaniel head, showing correct type and proportion.

legs do not paddle, wave or overlap. The head is held low when gaiting. The breed should be shown on a loose lead so that its natural gait is evident.

Temperament: Despite its somber and serious expression, the breed is friendly and has a cheerful and tractable disposition.

Faults: The standard ranks features of the breed into three categories. The most important features of the breed are color and general appearance. The features of secondary importance are the head, ears, back and back ribs, legs and feet. The features of lesser importance are the eyes, nose, neck, chest and shoulders, tail and coat. Faults also fall into three categories. Major faults are color that is too light or too dark, white on any part of the body other than the chest and a curled coat. Serious faults are a narrow head, weak muzzle, the presence of a topknot and a general appearance that is sour and crouching. Minor faults are light eyes, white on chest, the deviation from proper height ranges, lightness of bone, shortness of body or a body that is flat-sided and a bite other than scissors. There are no disqualifications in the Sussex Spaniel standard.

Color: Rich golden liver is the only acceptable color and is a certain sign of the purity of the breed. Dark liver or puce is a major fault. White on the chest is a minor fault. White on any other part of the body is a major fault.

Gait: The round, deep and wide chest of the Sussex Spaniel coupled with its short legs and long body produce a rolling gait. While its movement is deliberate, the Sussex Spaniel is in no sense clumsy. Gait is powerful and true with perfect coordination between the front and hind legs. The front

Approved April 7, 1992
Effective May 27, 1992

SUSSEX SPANIEL

HOW TO SELECT A PUPPY

In choosing a Sussex puppy, first and foremost consider your aspirations in acquiring a Sussex Spaniel. Do you wish to show your dog in the conformation ring? Do you want a superb bird dog? Do you want a household companion? Or, do you—as do many who choose the Sussex Spaniel—want a dog that can be all of these while wrapped in a sturdy golden liver wrapper?

While faults, such as legs that are overly long or a head style that varies too far from the standard, may effectively rule out a puppy as a show prospect, faults of this nature are not likely to make a difference for a Sussex Spaniel whose primary occupation will be as a hunting partner or household companion. Most Sussex Spaniel litters have an amount of variation among puppies in terms of type, personality and even size; it is extremely rare that all puppies in any single litter would be show prospects or that all puppies would show the interest in birds that is desirable in a hunting companion.

Know your goals before you begin contacting breeders; this will be helpful to the breeder in determining if there is an appropriate puppy for you in any particular litter. Speak to as many breeders as possible, in person, by telephone or by e-mail. This is an excellent way to become educated about the breed in general as well as about specific lines of dogs. Questions to ask include:

If you are looking for a potential competitor in the show ring or other events, look for titles in the pup's pedigree. This is Ch. Clussexx Harry Potter TD ("Harry").

Spaniel as a pet, does the breeder require that the puppy be spayed or neutered? Pet-quality animals should not be used in breeding programs and a responsible breeder will do all in his power to prevent unwise breeding of dogs from his line.

• Will the breeder provide you with a copy of a standard contract of sale, pictures of the sire and dam and proof of the sire's and dam's health clearances before requiring a deposit? What happens to the deposit if there is not a puppy in the litter that is right for you?

• How open is the breeder to answering questions from individuals who purchase puppies? You must feel comfortable with the person from whom you purchase your puppy.

• Is the breeder active in showing, hunting or other performance venues? If the breeder does not actively work with his animals in the show ring or performance, what is the reason that the individual is breeding?

• How does the breeder socialize his puppies? Are his puppies raised in a home or kennel?

• What does the breeder do if your life circumstances change and you can no longer keep your Sussex Spaniel?

• Can the breeder provide you with references of people who have purchased his puppies?

• If you are purchasing a Sussex

Once you know what your goals are in acquiring a puppy and have your questions well thought out, the next very important aspect to consider is overall health. After all, you will have this Sussex Spaniel for the next dozen or more years and nothing can break an owner's heart more quickly than a well-loved puppy that is not sound in body or mind.

SIGNS OF A HEALTHY PUPPY

Healthy puppies are robust little fellows who are alert and active, sporting shiny coats and supple skin. They should not appear lethargic, bloated or pot-bellied, nor should they have flaky skin or runny or crusted eyes or noses. Their stools should be firm and well formed, with no evidence of blood or mucus.

And, much to the dismay of concerned Sussex Spaniel breeders worldwide, even the most cautious breeding of two parents testing normal for all known "testable" problems may still produce a puppy who will show problems.

Sussex Spaniel breeders and potential owners are lucky in that the breed overall is a healthy one and that hereditary problems seen in the Sussex are relatively few. Nonetheless, it is important that breeders have their dogs tested for such problems, and it is important for prospective owners to inquire about the health of the breeder's line and to see documentation of the sire's and dam's test results. This includes eye certification from the Canine Eye Registration Foundation (CERF) and clearances from the Orthopedic Foundation for Animals, which has testing schemes for hip and elbow dysplasia, cardiac disease, thyroid disease and other hereditary problems. Hip dysplasia, hypothyroidism and eye and heart problems, as previously mentioned, are among the health issues to discuss with the breeder.

It is possible to get a feel for the general health of a breeder's stock by visiting the kennel if at all practical. Realistically, this is not always something that can be done, given the rarity of the breed and the various locations of breeders. For example, show

MAKE A COMMITMENT
Dogs are most assuredly man's best friend, but they are also a lot of work. When you add a puppy to your family, you also are adding to your daily responsibilities for years to come. Dogs need more than just food, water and a place to sleep. They also require training (which can be ongoing throughout the lifetime of the dog), activity to keep them physically and mentally fit and hands-on attention every day, plus grooming and health care. Your life as you now know it may well disappear! Are you prepared for such drastic changes?

prospects may be imported from one country to another. In some countries, such as the United States, obtaining a Sussex Spaniel puppy may mean not only a long, expectant wait but also the puppy's traveling by air from one coast to the other! To give you an idea of the breed's scarcity in the

US, only 29 Sussex Spaniel litters were registered by the AKC in 2005.

In cases where visiting the litter is not possible, you will need to do most of your investigation by telephone. Ask questions about the health, temperament and ages of the parents, and then go on to ask about the grandparents and great-grandparents; did these dogs live to older ages or did they die young? What health problems has the breeder encountered in previous litters? Be wary of any breeder who has bred more than a litter or two and who flatly states that he has never produced a dog with any sort of problem.

If you are fortunate enough to be able to visit the breeder, look at and interact with all of the dogs on the premises and assess their overall appearance, i.e., are these the type of dogs with which you wish to live? If you are too far away to make a visit, ask the breeder to send you photos or possibly videos of the parents, the

A family portrait of quality, winning Sussex Spaniels. This type of sound breeding is the type of line from which you should obtain your puppy.

PEDIGREE VS. REGISTRATION CERTIFICATE

Too often new owners are confused between these two important documents. Your puppy's pedigree, essentially a family tree, is a written record of a dog's genealogy of three generations or more. The pedigree will show you the names as well as performance titles of all dogs in your pup's background. Your breeder must provide you with a registration application, with his part properly filled out. You must complete the application and send it to the AKC with the proper fee. Every puppy must come from a litter that has been AKC-registered by the breeder, born in the US and from a sire and dam that are also registered with the AKC.

The seller must provide you with complete records to identify the puppy. The AKC requires that the seller provide the buyer with the following: breed; sex, color and markings; date of birth; litter number (when available); names and registration numbers of the parents; breeder's name; and date sold or delivered.

puppies, his other dogs, etc. Reviewing pedigrees can be helpful in some instances. For example, if your goal is a show dog with which to win in the conformation ring, check for champion titles over several generations of the pedigree. Similarly, if your goal is a hunting companion, look for evidence of proven hunting ability in the pedigree (such as field-trial titles).

If you are able to visit a litter in person, approach the visitation with your head and not your heart. The puppy that is extremely reticent may tug at your heart but may not be the best prospect if you have a busy household or if you wish to have a dog that virtually shouts "look at me" to a dog-show judge. On the other hand, this same puppy with a reserved but gentle nature may be the ideal companion in other situations.

Look for obvious signs of health: eyes should be clear without tearing; there should be no obvious structural problems such as lameness; there should be no coughing or raspiness to the breathing; coats should be shiny and healthy, etc. The overall litter simply should have the appearance of health and good nature—physically clean and accustomed to being handled by people.

Finally, inasmuch as you are interviewing the breeder, be prepared to have the breeder interview you! Sussex Spaniel breeders generally are a cautious lot and care deeply about placing each individual puppy in the most suitable home for that puppy. Be prepared for some in-depth questions about your home, your overall experience

with dogs and so forth. Give honest answers, as this will assist the breeder greatly in determining if there is a puppy in the litter that will suit your home and goals. A good match between an individual puppy and owner is essential to a happy dog-owner relationship.

A COMMITTED NEW OWNER
By now you should understand what makes the Sussex a most

GETTING ACQUAINTED
When visiting a litter, ask the breeder for suggestions on how best to interact with the puppies. If possible, get right into the middle of the pack and sit down with them. Observe which pups climb into your lap and which ones shy away. Toss a toy for them to chase and bring back to you. It's easy to fall in love with the first puppy who picks you, but keep your future objectives in mind before you make your final decision.

A lovely dam with her promising eight-week-old pup. Be sure to see at least the dam of your chosen pup, either in person or in photos/videos, as she will give you an idea of how your puppy will mature in looks, health and temperament.

pups falling somewhere in between. If you can spend time with the puppies, you will be able to recognize certain behaviors and what these behaviors indicate about each pup's temperament. Which type of pup will complement your family dynamics is best determined by observing the puppies in action within their "pack." Your breeder's expertise and recommendations are so valuable. Although you may fall in love with a bold and brassy male, the breeder may suggest that another pup would be best for you. The breeder's experience in rearing Sussex pups and matching their temperaments with appropriate humans offers

unique and special dog, one that may fit nicely into your family and lifestyle. If you have researched breeders, you should be able to recognize a knowledgeable and responsible Sussex Spaniel breeder who cares not only about his pups but also about what kind of owner you will be. If you have completed the next step in your exciting journey, you have found a litter, or possibly two, of quality Sussex pups.

Learning about the breeder and the puppies will be an education in itself. Breed research, breeder selection and puppy visitation are very important aspects of finding the puppy of your dreams. Beyond that, these things also lay the foundation for a successful future with your pup. Puppy personalities within each litter vary, from the shy and easygoing puppy to the one who is dominant and assertive, with most

SOME DAM ATTITUDE

When selecting a puppy, be certain to meet the dam of the litter. The temperament of the dam is often predictive of the temperament of her puppies. However, dams occasionally are very protective of their young, some to the point of being testy or aggressive with visitors, whom they may view as a danger to their babies. Such attitudes are more common when the pups are very young and still nursing and should not be mistaken for actual aggressive temperament. If possible, visit the dam away from her pups to make friends with her and gain a better understanding of her true personality.

the best assurance that your pup will meet your needs and expectations. The type of puppy that you select is just as important as your decision that the Sussex is the breed for you.

The decision to live with a Sussex is a serious commitment and not one to be taken lightly. This puppy is a living sentient being that will be dependent on you for basic survival for his entire life. Beyond the basics of survival—food, water, shelter and protection—he needs much, much more. The new pup needs love, nurturing and a proper canine education to mold him into a responsible, well-behaved canine citizen. Your Sussex Spaniel's health and good manners will need consistent monitoring and regular "tune-ups," so your job as a responsible dog owner will be ongoing throughout every stage of his life. If you are not prepared to accept these responsibilities and commit to them for the dog's entire lifetime then you are not prepared to own a dog of any breed.

Although the responsibilities of owning a dog may at times tax your patience, the joy of living with your Sussex far outweighs the workload, and a well-mannered adult dog is worth your time and effort. Before your very eyes, your new charge will grow up to be your most loyal friend, devoted to you unconditionally.

THE FAMILY TREE
Your puppy's pedigree is his family tree. Just as a child may resemble his parents and grandparents, so too will a puppy reflect the qualities, good and bad, of his ancestors, especially those in the first two generations. Therefore it's important to know as much as possible about a puppy's immediate relatives. Reputable and experienced breeders should be able to explain the pedigree and why they chose to breed from the particular dogs they used.

YOUR SUSSEX SHOPPING LIST
Just as expectant parents prepare a nursery for their baby, so should you ready your home for the arrival of your Sussex pup. If you have the necessary puppy supplies purchased and in place before he comes home, it will ease the puppy's transition from the warmth and familiarity of his mom and littermates to the brand-new environment of his new home and human family. You will

CREATE A SCHEDULE

Puppies thrive on sameness and routine. Offer meals at the same time each day, take him out at regular times for potty trips and do the same for play periods and outdoor activity. Make note of when your puppy naps and when he is most lively and energetic, and try to plan his day around those times. Once he is house-trained and more predictable in his habits, he will be better able to tolerate changes in his schedule.

be too busy to stock up and prepare your house after your pup comes home, that's for sure! Imagine how a pup must feel upon being transported to a strange new place. It's up to you to comfort him and to let your little pup know that he is going to be happy with you.

FOOD AND WATER BOWLS

Your puppy will need separate bowls for his food and water. Stainless steel pans are generally preferred over plastic bowls since they sterilize better and pups are less inclined to chew on the metal. Heavy-duty ceramic bowls are popular, but consider how often you will have to pick up those heavy bowls. Buy adult-sized pans, as your puppy will grow into them quickly.

Some breeders recommend feeding from elevated bowls, feeling that they provide a more natural feeding position. Elevated bowls also make a puppy "stretch up" and thus prevent him from bearing down on his front pasterns. Discuss the pros and cons of elevated bowls with your vet and breeder.

THE DOG CRATE

If you think that crates are tools of punishment and confinement for when a dog has misbehaved, think again. Most breeders and almost all trainers recommend a crate as the preferred house-train-

Aside from the myriad benefits of using a crate in the home, the crate is a must for safe travel. Show dogs are transported to and from shows in their crates, and the crates are used to safely confine the dogs as they await their turn in the ring.

ing aid as well as for all-around puppy training and safety. Because dogs are natural den creatures that prefer cave-like environ-

NEW RELEASES

Most breeders release their Sussex Spaniel puppies between eight to ten weeks of age. A breeder who allows puppies to leave the litter at five or six weeks of age is more concerned with profit than with the puppies' welfare. However, some breeders of show or working lines may hold one or more top-quality puppies longer in order to evaluate the Sussex Spaniel puppies' careers or show potential and decide which one(s) they will keep for themselves for showing, hunting and/or breeding.

ments, the benefits of crate use are many. The crate provides the puppy with his very own "safe house," a cozy place to sleep, take a break or seek comfort with a favorite toy; a travel aid to house your dog when on the road, at motels or at the vet's office; a training aid to help teach your puppy proper toileting habits; and a place of solitude when non-dog people happen to drop by and don't want a lively puppy—or even a well-behaved adult dog— saying hello or begging for attention.

Crates come in several types, although the wire crate and the fiberglass airline-type crate are the most popular. Both are safe and your puppy will adjust to either

Your Sussex Spaniel will, if properly trained, consider his crate as his private retreat.

Purchase a crate that will accommodate an adult Sussex. A medium-sized crate will suit most Sussex Spaniels. However, if your Sussex must be crated for any length of time, such as during the day when you are at work, a larger crate will be more comfortable for the dog.

The three most popular crate types: mesh on the left, wire on the right and fiberglass on top.

BEDDING AND CRATE PADS

Your puppy will enjoy some type of soft bedding in his "room" (the crate), something he can snuggle into to feel cozy and secure. Old towels or blankets are good choices for a young pup, since he may (and probably will) have a toileting accident or two in the crate or decide to chew on the bedding material. Once he is fully trained and out of the early

one, so the choice is up to you. The wire crates offer better visibility for the pup as well as better ventilation. Many of the wire crates easily fold into suitcase-size carriers. The fiberglass crates, similar to those used by the airlines for animal transport, are sturdier and more den-like. However, the fiberglass crates do not fold down and are less ventilated than the wire crates; this can be problematic in hot weather. Some of the newer crates are made of heavy plastic mesh; they are very lightweight and fold up into slim-line suitcases. However, a mesh crate might not be suitable for a pup with manic chewing habits.

Don't bother with a puppy-sized crate. Although your Sussex will be a small fellow when you bring him home, he will grow up in the blink of an eye and your puppy crate will be useless.

CRATE EXPECTATIONS

To make the crate more inviting to your puppy, you can offer his first meal or two inside the crate, always keeping the crate door open so that he does not feel confined. Keep a favorite toy or two in the crate for him to play with while inside. You can also cover the crate at night with a lightweight sheet to make it more den-like and remove the stimuli of household activity. Never put him into his crate as punishment or as you are scolding him, since he will then associate his crate with negative situations and avoid going there.

minds and bodies, puppies need toys to entertain their curious brains, wiggly paws and achy teeth. A fun array of safe doggie toys will help satisfy your puppy's chewing instincts and distract him from gnawing on the leg of your antique chair or your new leather sofa. Most puppy toys are cute and look as if they would be a lot of fun, but not all are necessarily safe or good for your puppy, so use caution when you go puppy-toy shopping.

During teething, the need to chew will escalate as expected with that developmental phenomenon. Sussex Spaniels who are bored also are known to resort to chewing to entertain themselves. It is up to the dog owner to provide appropriate chew items for the dog. An appropriate and generally inexpensive chew item is a raw beef shank (leg) bone, available from most butchers, in a length of 6 to 8 inches. Nylon bones and other similar sturdy man-made chew toys are also appropriate. Rawhide chews, chew hooves and other similar items are not advisable. Rawhide chews quickly become slimy, sticky messes, whereas chew hooves may break into sharp pieces when chewed. Both have been known to result in digestive ailments, sometimes requiring surgical intervention.

Soft woolly toys are special puppy favorites. They come in a

Your home and yard should be puppy-proofed before you bring your Sussex Spaniel home, as he'll be on the go and ready to explore!

chewing stage, you can replace the puppy bedding with a permanent crate pad if you prefer. Crate pads and other dog beds run the gamut from inexpensive to high-end doggie-designer styles, but don't splurge on the good stuff until you are sure that your puppy is reliable and won't tear it up or make a mess on it.

PUPPY TOYS

Just as infants and older children require objects to stimulate their

"I've got this tennis ball...is someone going to play with me?"

wide variety of cute shapes and sizes; some look like little stuffed animals. Puppies love to shake them up and toss them about or simply carry them around. Be careful of fuzzy toys that have button eyes or noses that your pup could chew off and swallow, and make sure that he does not disembowel a squeaky toy to remove the squeaker. Braided rope toys are similar in that they are fun to chew and toss around, but they shred easily and the strings are easy to swallow. The strings are not digestible and, if the puppy doesn't pass them in his stool, he could end up at the vet's office. Your puppy should be closely monitored with rope toys.

If you believe that your pup has ingested a piece of one of his toys, check his stools for the next couple of days to see if he passes the item when he defecates. At the same time, also watch for signs of intestinal distress. A call to your veterinarian might be in order to get his advice and be on the safe side.

An all-time favorite toy for puppies (young and old!) is the empty gallon milk jug. Hard plastic juice containers—46 ounces or more—are also excellent. Such containers make lots of noise when they are batted about, and puppies go crazy with delight as they play with them. However, they don't often last very long, so

TOYS 'R SAFE

The vast array of tantalizing puppy toys is staggering. Stroll through any pet shop or pet-supply outlet and you will see that the choices can be overwhelming. However, not all dog toys are safe or sensible. Most very young puppies enjoy soft woolly toys that they can snuggle with and carry around. (You know they have outgrown them when they shred them up!) Avoid toys that have buttons, tabs or other enhancements that can be chewed off and swallowed. Soft toys that squeak are fun, but make sure your puppy does not disembowel the toy and remove (and swallow) the squeaker. Toys that rattle or make noise can excite a puppy, but they present the same danger as the squeaky kind and so require supervision. Hard rubber toys that bounce can also entertain a pup, but make sure that the toy is too big for your pup to swallow.

snug enough that it won't slip off yet loose enough to be comfortable for the pup. You should be able to slip two fingers between the collar and his neck. Check the collar often, as puppies grow in spurts, and his collar can become too tight almost overnight. Choke collars are made for correcting a dog during training, but Sussex Spaniels do not react well to negative reinforcement; rather, their training should be based on positive, motivational methods with lots of praise.

Acclimating the pup to wearing a collar is an important basis of safety and training.

be sure to remove and replace them when they get chewed up.

A word of caution about homemade toys: be careful with your choices of non-traditional play objects. Never use old shoes or socks, since a puppy cannot distinguish between the old ones on which he's allowed to chew and the new ones in your closet that are strictly off limits. That principle applies to anything that resembles something that you don't want your puppy to chew.

COLLARS

A lightweight nylon collar is the best choice for a very young pup. Quick-click collars are easy to put on and remove, and they can be adjusted as the puppy grows. Introduce him to his collar as soon as he comes home to get him accustomed to wearing it. He'll get used to it quickly and won't mind a bit. Make sure that it is

LEASHES

A 6-foot nylon lead is an excellent choice for a young puppy. It is lightweight and not as tempting to chew as a leather lead. You can switch to a 6-foot leather lead after your pup has grown and is used to walking politely on a lead. For initial puppy walks and house-training purposes, you should invest in a shorter lead so that you have more control over the puppy. At first, you don't want him wandering too far away from you, and when taking him out for toileting you will want to keep him in the specific area chosen for his potty spot.

Once the puppy is heel-trained with a traditional leash, you can consider purchasing a retractable lead. A retractable lead is excellent for walking adult dogs that are already leash-wise. This type of lead allows the dog to roam farther away from you and explore a wider area when out walking, and also retracts when you need to keep him close to you.

HOME SAFETY FOR YOUR PUPPY

The importance of puppy-proofing cannot be overstated. In addition to making your house comfortable for your Sussex's arrival, you also must make sure that your house is safe for your puppy before you bring him home. There are countless hazards in the owner's personal living environment that a pup can sniff, chew, swallow or destroy. Many are obvious; others are not. Do a thorough advance house check to remove or

rearrange those things that could hurt your puppy, keeping any potentially dangerous items out of areas to which he will have access.

Electrical cords are especially dangerous, since puppies view them as irresistible chew toys. Unplug and remove all exposed cords or fasten them beneath baseboards where the puppy cannot reach them. Veterinarians and firefighters can tell you horror stories about electrical burns and house fires that resulted from puppy-chewed electrical cords. Consider this a most serious precaution for your puppy and the rest of your family.

Scout your home for tiny objects that might be seen at a pup's eye level. Keep medication bottles and cleaning supplies well out of reach, and do the same with waste baskets and other trash containers. It goes without saying that you should not use rodent

Provide proper chew toys to avoid your pup's finding something else more to his liking. Sticks are never recommended chew devices.

KEEP OUT OF REACH

Most dogs don't browse around your medicine cabinet, but accidents do happen! The drug acetaminophen, the active ingredient in certain popular over-the-counter pain relievers, can be deadly to dogs and cats if ingested in large quantities. Acetaminophen toxicity, caused by the dog's swallowing 15 to 20 tablets, can be manifested in abdominal pains within a day or two of ingestion, as well as liver damage. If you suspect your dog has swiped a bottle of medication, get the dog to the vet immediately so that the vet can induce vomiting and cleanse the dog's stomach.

TOXIC PLANTS
Plants are natural puppy magnets, but many can be harmful, even fatal, if ingested by a puppy or adult dog. Scout your yard and home interior and remove any plants, bushes or flowers that could be even mildly dangerous. It could save your puppy's life. You can obtain a complete list of toxic plants from your veterinarian, at the public library or by looking online.

poison or other toxic chemicals in any puppy area and that you must keep such containers safely locked up. You will be amazed at how many places a curious puppy can discover!

Once your house has cleared inspection, check your yard. A sturdy high fence, well embedded into the ground, will give your dog a safe place to play and potty. Sussex Spaniels are notorious problem solvers, and this includes turning their considerable attention to the activity of escaping confinement. While certainly not all Sussex Spaniels work to escape, there are enough stories of Sussex Spaniels' climbing and digging that pet owners must consider the potential.

The remedy is to make the fence well embedded into the ground (about 1 foot deep) and high enough so that it really is impossible for your dog to get over it. In general, a 4-foot-tall fence is adequate, though a 6-foot-tall fence is preferable. Some Sussex Spaniels who are persistent may require an escape-proof top cover on a kennel run. Check the fence or run periodically for necessary repairs. If there is a weak link or space to squeeze through, you can be sure a determined Sussex will discover it.

The garage and shed can be hazardous places for a pup, as things like fertilizers, chemicals and tools are usually kept there. It's best to keep these areas off limits to the pup. Antifreeze is especially dangerous to dogs, as they find the taste appealing and it takes only a few licks from the driveway to kill a dog, puppy or adult, small breed or large.

VISITING THE VETERINARIAN
A good veterinarian is your Sussex puppy's best health-insurance policy. If you do not already have a vet, ask friends and experienced dog people in your area for recommendations so that you can select

A Dog-Safe Home

The dog-safety police are taking you on a house tour. Let's go room by room and see how safe your own home is for your new Sussex Spaniel. The following items are doggy dangers, so either they must be removed or the dog should be monitored or not have access to these areas.

Outdoor
- swimming pool
- pesticides
- toxic plants
- lawn fertilizers

Living Room
- house plants (some varieties are poisonous)
- fireplace or wood-burning stove
- paint on the walls (lead-based paint is toxic)
- lead drapery weights (toxic lead)
- lamps and electrical cords
- carpet cleaners or deodorizers

Bathroom
- blue water in the toilet bowl
- medicine cabinet (filled with potentially deadly bottles)
- soap bars, bleach, drain cleaners, etc.
- tampons

Kitchen
- household cleaners in the kitchen cabinets
- glass jars and canisters
- sharp objects (like kitchen knives, scissors and forks)
- garbage can (with remnants of good-smelling things like onions, potato skins, apple or pear cores, peach pits, coffee beans, etc.)
- "people foods" that are toxic to dogs, like chocolate, raisins, grapes, nuts and onions

Garage
- antifreeze
- fertilizers (including rose foods)
- pesticides and rodenticides
- pool supplies (chlorine and other chemicals)
- oil and gasoline in containers
- sharp objects, electrical cords and power tools

a vet before you bring your Sussex puppy home. Also arrange for your puppy's first veterinary examination beforehand, since many vets do not have appointments immediately available and your puppy should visit the vet within a day or so of coming home.

It's important to make sure your puppy's first visit to the vet is a pleasant and positive one. The vet should take great care to befriend the pup and handle him gently to make their first meeting a positive experience. The vet will give the pup a thorough physical examination and set up a schedule for vaccinations and other necessary wellness visits. Be sure to show your vet any health and inoculation records, which you should have received from your breeder. Your vet is a great source of canine health information, so be sure to ask questions and take notes. Creating a health journal for your puppy will make a handy reference for his wellness and any future health problems that may arise.

MEETING THE FAMILY

Your Sussex's homecoming is an exciting time for all members of the family, and it's only natural that everyone will be eager to meet him, pet him and play with him. However, for the puppy's sake, it's best to make these initial family meetings as uneventful as possible so that the pup is not overwhelmed with too much too soon. Remember, he has just left his dam and his littermates and is away from the breeder's home for the first time. Despite his fuzzy wagging tail, he is still apprehensive and wondering where he is and who all these strange humans are. It's best to let him explore on his own and meet the family members as he feels comfortable. Let him investigate all the new smells, sights and sounds at his own pace. Children should be especially careful to not get overly excited, use loud voices or hug the pup too tightly. Be calm, gentle and affectionate, and be ready to comfort him if he appears frightened or uneasy.

ARE VACCINATIONS NECESSARY?

Vaccinations are recommended for all puppies by the American Veterinary Medical Association (AVMA). Some vaccines are absolutely necessary, while others depend upon a dog's or puppy's individual exposure to certain diseases or the animal's immune history. Rabies vaccinations are required by law in all 50 states. Some diseases are fatal whereas others are treatable, making the need for vaccinating against the latter questionable. Follow your veterinarian's recommendations to keep your dog fully immunized and protected. You can also review the AVMA directive on vaccinations on their website: www.avma.org.

Be sure to show your puppy his new crate during this first day home. Toss a treat or two inside the crate; if he associates the crate with food, he will associate the crate with good things. If he is comfortable with the crate, you can offer him his first meal inside it. Leave the door ajar so he can wander in and out as he chooses.

FIRST NIGHT IN HIS NEW HOME

So much has happened in your Sussex puppy's first day away from the breeder. He's likely had his first car ride to his new home. He's met his new human family and perhaps the other family pets. He has explored his new house and yard, at least those places where he is to be allowed during his first weeks at home. He may

have visited his new veterinarian. He has eaten his first meal or two away from his dam and litter-mates. Surely that's enough to tire out an eight-week-old Sussex pup—or so you hope!

It's bedtime. During the day, the pup investigated his crate, which is his new den and sleeping space, so it is not entirely strange to him. Line the crate with a soft towel or blanket that he can snuggle into and gently place him into the crate for the night. Some breeders send home a piece of bedding from where the pup slept with his littermates, and those familiar scents are a great comfort for the puppy on his first night without his siblings.

He will probably whine or cry. The puppy is objecting to the confinement and the fact that he is alone for the first time. This can be a stressful time for you as well as for the pup. It's important that you remain strong and don't let the puppy out of his crate to

Snuggling with mom is what your new puppy will miss most in his first few nights after leaving the breeder.

Bright-eyed and alert, this eight-week-old is ready to go to his new home and make the transition into his new family pack.

THE FIRST FAMILY MEETING

Your puppy's first day at home should be quiet and uneventful. Despite his wagging tail, he is still wondering where his mom and siblings are! Let him make friends with other members of the family on his own terms; don't overwhelm him. You have a lifetime ahead to get to know each other!

comfort him. He will fall asleep eventually. If you release him, the puppy will learn that crying means "out" and will continue that habit. You are laying the groundwork for future habits. Some breeders find that soft music can soothe a crying pup and help him get to sleep.

SOCIALIZING YOUR PUPPY

The first 20 weeks of your Sussex puppy's life are the most important of his entire lifetime. A properly socialized puppy will grow up to be a confident and stable adult who will be a pleasure to live with and a welcome addition to the neighborhood.

The importance of socialization cannot be overemphasized. Research on canine behavior has proven that puppies who are not exposed to new sights, sounds, people and animals during their first 20 weeks of life will grow up to be timid and fearful, even aggressive, and unable to flourish outside of their familiar home environment.

Socializing your puppy is not difficult and, in fact, will be a fun time for you both. Lead training goes hand in hand with socialization, so your puppy will be learning how to walk on a lead at the same time that he's meeting the neighborhood. Because the Sussex is such a terrific breed, everyone will enjoy meeting "the new kid on the block." Take him for short walks to the park and to other dog-friendly places where he will encounter new people, especially children. Puppies automatically recognize children as "little people" and are drawn to play with them. Just make sure that you supervise these meetings and that the children do not get too rough or encourage him to play too hard. An overzealous pup can often nip too hard, frightening the child and in turn making the puppy overly excited. A bad experience in puppyhood can impact a dog for life, so a pup that has a negative experience with a child may grow up to be shy or even aggressive around children.

Take your puppy along on your daily errands. Puppies are natural "people magnets," and most people who see your pup will want to pet him. All of these encounters will help to mold him into a confident adult dog. Likewise, you will soon feel like a confident, responsible dog owner, rightly proud of your mannerly Sussex Spaniel.

Be especially careful of your puppy's encounters and experiences during the eight-to-ten-week-old period, which is also called the "fear period." This is a serious imprinting period, and all contact during this time should be gentle and positive. A frightening or negative event could leave a permanent impression that could affect his future behavior if a similar situation arises.

Also make sure that your puppy has received his first and second rounds of vaccinations before you expose him to other dogs or bring him to places that other dogs may frequent. Avoid dog parks and other strange-dog areas until your vet assures you that your puppy is fully immunized and resistant to the diseases that can be passed between canines. Discuss safe early socialization with your breeder and vet, as some recommend socializing the puppy even before he has received all of his inoculations, depending on the puppy.

LEADER OF THE PUPPY'S PACK
Like other canines, your puppy needs an authority figure, someone he can look up to and regard as the leader of his "pack." His first pack leader was his dam, who taught him to be polite and not chew too hard on her ears or nip at her muzzle. He learned

those same lessons from his littermates. If he played too rough, they cried in pain and stopped the game, which sent an important message to the rowdy puppy.

As puppies play together, they are also struggling to determine

THE CRITICAL SOCIALIZATION PERIOD
Canine research has shown that a puppy's 8th through 20th week is the most critical learning period of his life. This is when the puppy "learns to learn," a time when he needs positive experiences to build confidence and stability. Puppies who are not exposed to different people and situations outside the home during this period can grow up to be fearful and sometimes aggressive. This is also the best time for puppy lessons, since he has not yet acquired any bad habits that could undermine his ability to learn.

who will be the boss. Being pack animals, dogs need someone to be in charge. If a litter of puppies remained together beyond puppyhood, one of the pups would emerge as the strongest one, the one who calls the shots.

Once your puppy leaves the pack, he will look intuitively for a new leader. If he does not recognize you as that leader, he will try to assume that position for himself. Of course, it is hard to imagine your adorable Sussex puppy trying to be in charge when he is so small and seemingly helpless. You must remember that these are natural canine instincts. Do not cave in and allow your pup to get the upper "paw"!

Just as socialization is so important during these first 20 weeks, so too is your puppy's early education. He was born without any bad habits. He does not know what is good or bad behavior. If he does things like nipping and digging, it's because he is having fun and doesn't know that humans consider these things as "bad." It's your job to teach him proper puppy manners, and this is the best time to accomplish that—before he has developed bad habits, since it is much more difficult to "unlearn" or correct unacceptable learned behavior than to teach good behavior from the start.

Make sure that all members of the family understand the importance of being consistent when training their new puppy. If you tell the puppy to stay off the sofa and your daughter allows him to cuddle on the couch to watch her favorite television show, your pup will be confused about what he is and is not allowed to do. Have a family conference before your pup comes home so that everyone understands the basic principles of puppy training and the rules you have set forth for the pup and agrees to follow them.

The old saying that "an ounce of prevention is worth a pound of cure" is especially true when it comes to puppies. It is much easier to prevent inappropriate behavior than it is to change it. It's also easier and less stressful for the pup, since it will keep discipline to a minimum and create a more positive learning environment for him. That, in turn, will also be easier on you.

CONFINEMENT

It is wise to keep your puppy confined to a small "puppy-proofed" area of the house for his first few weeks at home. Gate or block off a space near the door he will use for outdoor potty trips. Expandable baby gates are useful to create your puppy's designated area. If he is allowed to roam through the entire house or even only several rooms, it will be more difficult to house-train him.

HAPPY PUPPIES COME RUNNING

Never call your puppy (or adult dog) to come to you and then scold him or discipline him when he gets there. He will make a natural association between coming to you and being scolded, and he will think he was a bad dog for coming to you. He will then be reluctant to come whenever he is called. Always praise your puppy every time he comes to you.

Here are a few commonsense tips to keep your belongings safe and your puppy out of trouble:

- Keep your closet doors closed and your shoes, socks and other apparel off the floor so your puppy can't get to them.
- Keep a secure lid on the trash container or put the trash where your puppy can't dig into it. He can't damage what he can't reach!
- Supervise your puppy at all times to make sure he is not getting into mischief. If he starts to chew the corner of the rug, you can distract him instantly by tossing a toy for him to fetch. You also will be able to whisk him outside when you notice that he is about to piddle on the carpet. If you can't see your puppy, you can't teach him or correct his behavior.

SOLVING PUPPY PROBLEMS

CHEWING AND NIPPING

Nipping at fingers and toes is normal puppy behavior. Chewing is also the way that puppies investigate their surroundings. However, you will have to teach your puppy that chewing anything other than his toys is not acceptable. That won't happen overnight and at times puppy teeth will test your patience. However, if you allow nipping and chewing to continue, just think about the damage that a mature Sussex can do with a full set of adult teeth.

Whenever your puppy nips your hand or fingers, cry out "Ouch!" in a loud voice, which should startle your puppy and stop him from nipping, even if only for a moment. Immediately distract him by offering a small treat or an appropriate toy for him to chew instead (which means having chew toys and puppy treats handy or in your pockets at all times). Praise him when he takes the toy and tell him what a good fellow he is. Praise is just as or even more important in puppy training as discipline and correction.

Puppies also tend to nip at children more often than adults, since they perceive little ones to be more vulnerable and more similar to their littermates. Teach your children appropriate

Ankles and trouser legs are at just the right height to satisfy a pup's urge to nip. This behavior must be consistently discouraged as soon as it begins.

coming in. At this stage, chewing just plain feels good. Furniture legs and cabinet corners are common puppy favorites. Shoes and other personal items also taste pretty good to a pup.

The best solution is, once again, prevention. If you value something, keep it tucked away and out of reach. You can't hide your dining-room table in a closet, but you can try to deflect the chewing by applying a bitter product made just to deter dogs from chewing. Available in a spray or cream, this substance is vile-tasting, although safe for dogs, and most puppies will avoid the forbidden object after one tiny taste. You also can apply the product to your leather leash if the puppy tries to chew on his lead during leash-training sessions.

Keep a ready supply of safe chews handy to offer your Sussex as a distraction when he starts to chew on something that's a "no-no." Remember, at this tender age, he does not yet know what is permitted or forbidden, so you have to be "on call" every minute he's awake and on the prowl.

You may lose a treasure or two during your puppy's growing-up period, and the furniture could sustain a nasty nick or two. These can be trying times, so be prepared for those inevitable accidents and comfort yourself in knowing that this too shall pass.

responses to nipping behavior. If they are unable to handle it themselves, you may have to intervene. Puppy nips can be quite painful and a child's frightened reaction will only encourage a puppy to nip harder, which is a natural canine response. As with all other puppy situations, interaction between your Sussex puppy and children should be supervised.

Chewing on objects, not just family members' fingers and ankles, is also normal canine behavior that can be especially tedious (for the owner, not the pup) during the teething period when the puppy's adult teeth are

PUPPY WHINING

Puppies often cry and whine, just as infants and little children do. It's their way of telling us that they are lonely or in need of attention. Your puppy will miss his littermates and will feel insecure when he is left alone. You may be out of the house or just in another room, but he will still feel alone. During these times, the puppy's crate should be his personal comfort station, a place all his own where he can feel safe and secure. Once he learns that being alone is okay and not something to be feared, he will settle down without crying or objecting. You might want to leave a radio on while he is crated, as the sound of human voices can be soothing and will give the impression that people are around.

Give your puppy a favorite cuddly toy or chew toy to entertain him whenever he is crated. You will both be happier: the puppy because he is safe in his den and you because he is quiet, safe and not getting into puppy escapades that can wreak havoc in your house or cause him danger.

To make sure that your puppy will always view his crate as a safe and cozy place, never, ever use the crate as punishment. That's the best way to turn the crate into a negative place that the pup will want to avoid. Sure, you can use the crate for your own peace of mind if your puppy is getting into trouble and needs some "time out." Just don't let him know that! Never scold the pup and immediately place him into the crate. Count to ten, give him a couple of hugs and maybe a treat, then scoot him into his crate.

It's also important not to make a big fuss when he is released from the crate. That will make getting out of the crate more appealing than being in the crate, which is just the opposite of what you are trying to achieve.

THE FAMILY FELINE

A resident cat has feline squatter's rights. The cat will treat the newcomer (your puppy) as she sees fit, regardless of what you do or say. So it's best to let the two of them work things out on their own terms. Cats have a height advantage and will generally leap to higher ground to avoid direct contact with a rambunctious pup. Some will hiss and boldly swat at a pup who passes by or tries to reach the cat. Keep the puppy under control in the presence of the cat and they will eventually become accustomed to each other.

Here's a hint: move the cat's litter box where the puppy can't get into it! It's best to do so well before the pup comes home so the cat is used to the new location.

PROPER CARE OF YOUR

SUSSEX SPANIEL

Adding a Sussex to your household means adding a new family member who will need your care each and every day. When your Sussex pup first comes home, you will start a routine with him so that, as he grows up, your dog will have a daily schedule just as you do. The aspects of your dog's daily care will likewise become regular parts of your day, so you'll both have a new schedule. Dogs learn by consistency and thrive on routine: regular times for meals, exercise, grooming and potty trips are just as important for your dog as they are for you! Your dog's schedule will depend much on your family's daily routine, but remember that you now have a new member of the family who is part of your day every day.

FEEDING

Feeding your dog the best diet is based on various factors, including age, activity level, overall condition and size of breed. When you visit the breeder, he will share with you his advice about the proper diet for your dog based on his experience with the breed and the foods with which he has had success. Likewise, your vet will be a helpful source of advice throughout the dog's life and will aid you in planning a diet for optimal health.

FEEDING THE PUPPY

Of course, your pup's very first food will be his dam's milk. There may be special situations in which pups fail to nurse, necessitating that the breeder hand-feed them with a formula, but for the most part pups spend the first weeks of life nursing from their dam. The

JUST ADD MEAT

An organic alternative to the traditional dog kibble or canned food comes in the form of grain-based feeds. These dry cereal-type products consist of oat and rye flakes, corn meal, wheat germ, dried kelp and other natural ingredients. The manufacturers recommend that the food be mixed with meat in a ratio of two parts grain to one part meat. As an alternative to fresh meat, investigate freeze-dried meat and fermented meat products, which makers claim are more nutritious and digestible for dogs.

breeder weans the pups by gradually introducing solid foods and decreasing the milk meals. Pups may even start themselves off on the weaning process, albeit inadvertently, if they snatch bites from their mom's food bowl.

By the time the pups are ready for new homes, they are fully weaned and eating a good puppy food. As a new owner, you may be thinking, "Great! The breeder has taken care of the hard part." Not so fast.

A puppy's first year of life is the time when all or most of his growth and development takes place. This is a delicate time, and diet plays a huge role in proper skeletal and muscular formation. Improper diet and exercise habits can lead to damaging problems that will compromise the dog's health and movement for his entire life.

Veterinarians often recommend that puppies be maintained on a food formulated for puppies until one year of age, but this is *not* ideal for Sussex Spaniels. Food formulated specifically for puppies often encourages a rate of growth in body mass (weight) that outpaces the strength of musculature and other soft-tissue support structures. The result is that the front assembly of the dog suffers.

Feed the puppy a good-quality adult dog food. The Sussex Spaniel puppy should be lean. Like the gawky human adolescent,

the appearance should portend that there is much more to come as the frame slowly fills out with maturity. The Sussex Spaniel is not a small spaniel by any means, and puppies that mature too quickly may not develop the overall size and substance typical for the breed.

Many Sussex Spaniel owners have had considerable success with natural diets for their companions following the recommendations of any one of several reputable authors to assure that the diet is balanced. It is always wise to consult the breeder of your puppy about specific feeding practices.

Because of a young pup's small body and accordingly small digestive system, his daily portion

Knowing what and how to feed your new Sussex Spaniel puppy are questions to be answered before the pup comes home. Take advice from the breeder, who is knowledgeable about what works best with his line of dogs.

will be divided up into small meals throughout the day. This can mean starting off with three or more meals a day and decreasing the number of meals as the pup matures. Eventually you can feed only one meal a day, although it is generally thought that dividing the day's food into two meals on a morning/evening schedule is healthier for the dog's digestion.

Regarding the feeding schedule, feeding the pup at the same times and in the same place each day is important for both housebreaking purposes and establishing the dog's everyday routine. As for the amount to feed, growing puppies generally need proportion-ately more food per body weight than their adult counterparts, but a pup should never be allowed to gain excess weight. Dogs of all ages should be kept in proper body condition, but extra weight can strain a pup's developing frame, causing skeletal problems.

Watch your pup's weight as he grows and, if the recommended amounts seem to be too much or too little for your pup, consult the vet about appropriate dietary changes. Keep in mind that treats, although small, can quickly add up throughout the day, contributing unnecessary calories. Treats are fine when used prudently; opt for dog treats specially formulated to be healthy or for nutritious snacks like small pieces of cheese or cooked chicken.

FEEDING THE ADULT DOG

A dog generally is considered an adult when it has stopped growing. The Sussex Spaniel is a slow-maturing breed, with full maturity often not seen until three years of age. While the one-year-old Sussex Spaniel may have reached his full height, substantial changes can and do occur in body substance and both in amount and length of coat. You should feed the adult Sussex on a high-quality adult food, relying on the breeder or your veterinarian to recommend an acceptable maintenance diet.

For the adult (meaning physically mature) dog, feeding

VARIETY IS THE SPICE

Although dog-food manufacturers contend that dogs don't like variety in their diets, studies show quite the opposite to be true. Dogs would much rather vary their meals than eat the same old chow day in and day out. Dry kibble is no more exciting for a dog than the same bowl of bran flakes would be for you. Fortunately, there are dozens of varieties available on the market, and your dog will likely show preference for certain flavors over others. A word of warning: don't overdo it or you'll develop a fussy eater who only prefers chopped beef fillet and asparagus tips every night.

SUPPLEMENTATION

While excessive supplementation is not recommended, there are some supplements commonly used by Sussex Spaniel fanciers.

Kelp: a supplement to enhance overall immune system function and improve coat, which is used by a number of fanciers.

Vitamin C: this water-soluble vitamin is often used during major growth phases, typically until the puppy reaches two years of age.

Omega Fatty Acid supplements: these oils are often useful, particularly with liver-colored coats, which tend to be somewhat drier and less glossy than coats of other colors.

Other supplements used vary widely, according to individual preference of the breeder. It is best to consult with the breeder of your puppy and to follow the feeding instructions given.

overall daily caloric intake, and avoid offering table scraps. Overweight dogs are more prone to health problems. Research has even shown that obesity takes years off a dog's life. With that in mind, resist the urge to overfeed and over-treat. Don't make unnecessary additions to your dog's diet, whether with tidbits or with extra vitamins and minerals.

The amount of food needed for proper maintenance will vary depending on the individual dog's activity level, but you will be able to tell whether the daily portions are keeping him in good shape. With the wide variety of good complete foods available, choosing what to feed is largely a matter of personal preference. Just as with the puppy, the adult dog should have consistency in his mealtimes and feeding place. In addition to a consistent routine, regular mealtimes also allow the owner to see how much his dog is eating. If the

Puppies can be messy eaters and drinkers. This breeder uses newspapers to help keep the pups' area clean.

properly is about maintenance, not growth. Again, correct weight is a concern. Your dog should appear fit and should have an evident "waist." His ribs should not be protruding (a sign of being underweight), but they should be covered by only a slight layer of fat. Under normal circumstances, an adult dog can be maintained fairly easily with a high-quality nutritionally complete adult-formula food.

Factor treats into your dog's

dog seems never to be satisfied or, likewise, becomes uninterested in his food, the owner will know right away that something is wrong and can consult the vet.

DIETS FOR THE AGING DOG

Sussex Spaniels have a lifespan of approximately 12 years of age (usually ranging between 11 and 15 years of age). The typical age at which a dog is considered a "senior" varies greatly. The shift, if any, from adult to senior dog food should be made based on the needs of the individual animal rather than on age. Seniors often may continue to be fed regular adult dog food with no ill effects. Others, particularly those who are less active or those with weight-control problems, may do better with smaller portions or with a senior food that has fewer calories per cup of dry weight. Watching the dog's weight remains essential, even more so in the senior stage. Older dogs are already more vulnerable to illness, and obesity only contributes to their susceptibility to problems.

For seniors with specific medical problems, special diets may be needed as recommended by your vet. Be sensitive to your senior Sussex Spaniel's diet, as this will help control other problems that may arise with your old friend. As with any other changes, you should consult your vet for advice before making changes to your Sussex's diet.

QUENCHING HIS THIRST

Is your dog drinking more than normal and trying to lap up everything in sight? Excessive drinking has many different causes. Obvious causes for a dog's being thirstier than usual are hot weather and vigorous exercise. However, if your dog is drinking more for no apparent reason, you could have cause for concern. Serious conditions like kidney or liver disease, diabetes and various types of hormonal problems can all be indicated by excessive drinking. If you notice your dog's being excessively thirsty, contact your vet at once. Hopefully there will be a simpler explanation, but the earlier a serious problem is detected, the sooner it can be treated, with a better rate of cure.

Don't Forget the Water!

For a dog, it's always time for a drink! Regardless of what type of food he eats, there's no doubt that he needs plenty of water. Fresh cold water, in a clean bowl, should be freely available to your dog at all times. There are special circumstances, such as during puppy housebreaking, when you will want to monitor your pup's water intake so that you will be able to predict when he will need to relieve himself, but water must be available to him nonetheless. Water is essential for hydration and proper body function just as it is in humans.

You will get to know how much your dog typically drinks in a day. Of course, in the heat or if exercising vigorously, he will be more thirsty and will drink more. However, if he begins to drink noticeably more water for no apparent reason, this could signal any of various problems, and you are advised to consult your vet.

Water is the best drink for dogs. Some owners are tempted to give milk from time to time or to moisten dry food with milk, but dogs do not have the enzymes necessary to digest the lactose in milk, which is much different from the milk that nursing puppies receive. Therefore stick with clean fresh water to quench your dog's thirst, and always have it readily available to him.

EXERCISE

The Sussex Spaniel's exercise needs vary greatly among individuals. Sussex Spaniels from lines bred not only for conformation but also for working ability (hunting, obedience, agility, tracking) will typically need more exercise than those from lines bred primarily for the conformation show ring with less emphasis on performance. On the average, a couple of brisk 15- to 20-minute walks each day, or at least daily sessions of throwing a tennis ball or retrieving a bumper in the yard, are recommended.

Creating a safe place for a Sussex Spaniel puppy to play freely, such as a fenced yard, is helpful to allow the puppy to exercise to the amount that the puppy requires. That being said, all Sussex Spaniels need quality exercise that includes interaction and playtime with their human companions; this is not a breed that will be content to be relegated to the yard without human interaction.

Exercise time is fun for dogs and owner, as it provides all concerned with needed activity and important opportunities for bonding.

Harry sits patiently on the grooming table before a show, getting ready for his appearance in the ring.

Bear in mind that an overweight dog should never be suddenly over-exercised; instead he should be encouraged to increase exercise slowly. Also, not only is exercise essential to keep the dog's body fit, it is essential to his mental well-being. A bored dog will find something to do, which often manifests itself in some type of destructive behavior.

GROOMING

The Sussex Spaniel is very much a "wash and wear" breed. While grooming for the show ring has considerable variations from country to country, there are basic grooming procedures that are necessary for the overall health and well-being of the Sussex Spaniel as well as for maintaining a typical appearance. The basic grooming described here is for the household companion. There is a bit more to learn for grooming a show dog, and your dog's breeder is often your very best source of information for learning the requirements of show grooming.

BRUSHING AND COMBING

Most Sussex Spaniels absolutely enjoy time with their owners, including time spent being brushed and combed. After all, it is a time when your Sussex has your undivided attention, and regular grooming sessions can be very relaxing for both you and your dog. On at least a weekly basis, use the bristle brush, starting at the top of the skull and working toward the tail, always going with the lay of the hair. Avoid brushing the facial area; use a barely damp towel to groom this area, again always going with the lay of the hair.

Sussex Spaniels do shed. Brushing removes dead hair and, with regular brushing, you will see far less shedding in the form of "fluff balls" of dog hair drifting into corners. A conditioning grooming spray may be used during brushing; this is particularly helpful for dogs that will be shown in the conformation ring, as it helps prevent coat breakage.

Following brushing, use the comb for feathering on the ears, legs and belly area. Gently work out any tangles that might be present to avoid any discomfort to your dog. If needed, depending on how much time your Sussex Spaniel spends outdoors, a sunscreen spray is helpful to apply as a final mist to prevent bleaching of the coat, which is particularly a problem for liver-colored dogs like the Sussex.

TRIMMING

Neatening up the haircoat is helpful in maintaining a typical Sussex Spaniel appearance, whether the dog is a household companion or show dog. Trimming, even for the show ring, should only enhance the natural appearance of the dog. The choice of tools to use for trimming the coat varies considerably among fanciers. It is safe to say that the stripping knife is utilized worldwide to remove dead coat as well as to blend coat or remove excessive length, while the straight shear is used to shorten the hair on the back of the rear legs from hock to ground. The straight shear also should be used carefully to trim hair from the footpads so that the dog is not walking on hair, thereby losing the natural traction supplied by the pads.

In general, the hair on the upper one-third of the outer ear is shortened to enhance the appearance of the set of the ear, allowing the ear to gracefully frame the face. This may be accomplished by use of the stripping knife or thinning shear, both to shorten as necessary and to blend the hair to lie flat and create a gradual transition of the hair from skull to ear to

SUSSEX GROOMING TOOLS

There are variations in methods for trimming and preparing the dog for the show ring among fanciers in different countries. Regardless, the basic grooming equipment needed includes the following:
• Bristle brush (natural bristle-style recommended)
• "Greyhound"-style comb
• Straight shears
• Stripping knife
• Shampoo formulated for canines
• Hand towel or face flannel
• Hand-held hair dryer
• Nail clipper and nail file or nail grinder
• Styptic powder or liquid
• Ear cleanser, powder or liquid as recommended by your vet or breeder
• Cotton wipes and cotton balls
• Soft toothbrush and canine toothpaste or other dental-care products as recommended by the vet or breeder
• Thinning shears (optional)
• Grooming spray for daily use (optional)
• Grooming table (optional)
• Coat conditioner for use after bathing (optional)
• SPF-rated sun protection spray for coat (optional)

Carefully brush through the body coat. Using a grooming table will make grooming more comfortable for both dog and owner.

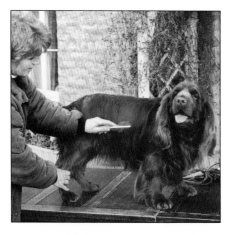

A comb-through following brushing will help to remove dead hair and ensure that the coat is mat- and tangle-free.

Don't forget the feathering, such as that on the ears. A comb should be used carefully and gently to detangle these areas.

neck. Hair from the lower jaw, an area about two finger-breadths above the prosternum of the chest, may also be shortened with a stripping knife to enhance the neckline of the dog. Again, the key is to remove just enough hair to neaten the appearance and blend well into the longer body coat. Excessive facial hair may be carefully stripped by using a small stripping knife created expressly for that purpose.

The stripping knife is the preferred tool to use on the body coat to remove fuzzy hair as commonly seen on liver-colored dogs. An electric clipper or thinning shear should never be used on the body coat, as doing so will often ruin the proper texture of the coat. As an alternative to the stripping knife, hand plucking of the body coat may be done. Though this is very time-consuming and can take a bit of practice to master, the end result is that the coat texture is truly enhanced in the best way.

BATHING

The frequency of bathing will depend greatly on the sort of activities done by the dog as well as on the coat of the individual dog. Some Sussex Spaniels have coats that are oilier than others, and these may become "doggy" more quickly. Therefore, if your Sussex Spaniel is a household companion and sleeps on your bed, you may wish to freshen your dog up a bit more often. Sussex Spaniels who are shown are often bathed far more frequently, particularly during show season. On the average, a home companion will require bathing no more frequently than once a month, especially if routine coat care via thorough brushing is done.

Brush your Sussex Spaniel thoroughly before wetting his coat. This will get rid of most mats and tangles, which are harder to remove when the coat is wet. Make certain that your dog has a good non-slip surface on which to stand. Before wetting the dog, place a cotton ball in the outer ears to prevent water from getting into the ear canals. Using tepid water, just warm to the touch, thoroughly wet the dog, beginning at the head and working toward the tail and from the top of the head to the feet. Apply dog shampoo as directed on the bottle, but avoid the face while doing so to prevent any irritation to the sensitive eyes. The face is cleansed easily using a damp face flannel. There are a vast number of shampoo formulations available for dogs, some of which are medicated for use with specific coat and skin problems. The mildest shampoo is often the best to avoid stripping the coat of essential oils, particularly with the Sussex and his liver-colored coat.

Work the shampoo all the way down to the skin. You can use this

WATER SHORTAGE

No matter how well behaved your dog is, bathing is always a project! Nothing can substitute for a good warm bath, but owners do have the option of giving their dogs "dry" baths. Pet shops sell excellent products, in both powder and spray forms, designed for spot-cleaning your dog. These dry shampoos are convenient for touch-up jobs when you don't have the time to bathe your dog in the traditional way.

Muddy feet, messy behinds and smelly coats can be spot-cleaned and deodorized with a "wet-nap"-style cleaner. On those days when your dog insists on rolling in fresh goose droppings and there's no time for a bath, a spot bath can save the day. These pre-moistened wipes are also handy for other grooming needs like wiping faces, ears and eyes and freshening tails and behinds.

opportunity to check the skin for any bumps, bites or other abnormalities. Do not neglect any area of the body—get all of the hard-to-reach places. After thoroughly lathering the dog, paying attention to the leg, belly and ear feathering, the dog should be rinsed thoroughly with tepid water. A spray device, such as one used for showering, makes the job of rinsing the dog much easier to do. Once again, be careful that no shampoo or soapy water gets near the dog's

Clean carefully around the eyes to remove any dirt or debris that can collect there, using a soft wipe and special cleanser.

Never probe into the ear canal. Clean your Sussex Spaniel's outer ears with a cotton wipe and ear powder or liquid made for dogs.

Weekly brushing of your Sussex Spaniel's teeth between visits to the vet is highly recommended.

eyes. It is essential that all traces of shampoo be removed, as leaving any shampoo in the coat will attract dirt as well as potentially irritate the skin.

When removing your Sussex from the bath, be prepared for him to shake out his coat—you might want to stand back, but make sure you have a hold on the dog to keep him from running through the house. Following rinsing, it is essential to dry the haircoat. A hand-held hair dryer on the low heat setting works quite well. Take care to direct the flow of air away from the face and to maintain a safe distance between the hair dryer and the dog. When the coat is dry, use the bristle brush for the body coat and use the comb to smooth out the feathering.

It is helpful to apply a coat conditioner, according to package directions, to accompany the final brushing after drying the dog. Just as a conditioning rinse is helpful to styling your own hair without tangles, coat conditioner works with the Sussex Spaniel's feathering.

EAR CLEANING

The beautiful ears of the Sussex Spaniel do require routine care. Routine care of the ears goes a long way toward preventing ear infections in this breed with pendulous ears, as the weight and length of the ears effectively cloak the ear openings, thereby creating an ideal dark, moist environment for infection. Ears should be cleaned weekly, using cotton wipes and a powder or liquid cleansing agent as recommended by your vet or breeder. Do not be tempted to use a cotton swab rather than a cotton wipe. It is far too easy to probe into the ear with a cotton swab and cause harm.

It is recommended that the hair around the ear openings be shortened by plucking or careful use of a thinning shear. This will keep the ears as dry as possible, particularly for Sussex Spaniels who will do a bit of swimming.

EYE CARE

During grooming sessions, pay extra attention to the condition of your dog's eyes. If the area around the eyes is soiled or if tear staining has occurred, there are various cleaning agents made especially for this purpose. Look at the dog's eyes to make sure no debris has entered; dogs with large eyes and those who spend time outdoors are especially prone to this.

The signs of an eye infection are obvious: mucus, redness, puffiness, scabs or other signs of irritation. If your dog's eyes become infected, the vet will likely prescribe an antibiotic ointment for treatment. If you notice signs of more serious problems, such as opacities in the eye, which usually indicate cataracts, consult the vet at once. Taking time to pay atten-

tion to your dog's eyes will alert you in the early stages of any problem so that you can get your dog treatment as soon as possible. You could save your dog's sight!

NAIL CLIPPING

Sussex Spaniels generally have tough, dark toenails and the "quick" (vascular nail bed) is nearly impossible to see. Nails must be maintained on a weekly basis, as nails that are too long may result in improper placement

SCOOTING HIS BOTTOM

Here's a doggy problem that many owners tend to neglect. If your dog is scooting his rear end around the carpet, he probably is experiencing anal-sac impaction or blockage. The anal sacs are the two grape-sized glands on either side of the dog's vent. The dog cannot empty these glands, which become filled with a foul-smelling material. The dog may attempt to lick the area to relieve the pressure. He may also rub his anus on your walls, furniture or floors.

Don't neglect your dog's rear end during grooming sessions. By squeezing both sides of the anus with a soft cloth, you can express some of the material in the sacs. If the material is pasty and thick, you likely will need the assistance of a veterinarian. Vets know how to express the glands and can show you how to do it correctly without hurting the dog or spraying yourself with the unpleasant liquid.

In addition to nail care, trimming the hair between the footpads will add to the foot's neat appearance as well as the dog's comfort.

of the foot as the nail hits the floor. A nail clipper is used to nip off the end of the nail, followed by using a nail file to smooth rough edges. Styptic powder is a necessity since, with the difficulty of seeing where the nail bed is, it is all too easy to cut a bit too close. As an alternative, a nail grinder may be utilized to shorten the nail while providing the same smoothing effect of the file at the same time.

Many dogs dislike nail cutting intensely. This may be avoided by routinely handling the feet at times other than nail cutting. Also, your Sussex Spaniel should be accustomed to having his nails trimmed at an early age, since nail clipping will be a part of your maintenance routine throughout

Heavy-duty canine nail clippers will be needed for you to clip your Sussex Spaniel's nails at home.

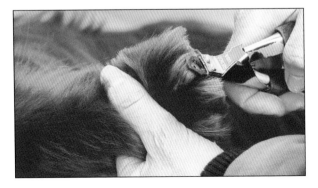

his life. If the puppy is accustomed to the procedure, he should grow up to tolerate it as an adult.

TOOTH CARE

Tartar build-up can be problematic, so routine care of the mouth is important to prevent tooth decay and gum disease. Weekly attention to the teeth is helpful in maintaining them in the best possible manner. While providing chew bones is helpful for removing tartar build-up naturally as the dog gnaws, this is not sufficient on its own. Use tooth-care products made for dogs (not people), available from your vet or pet-supply store.

IDENTIFICATION AND TRAVEL

ID FOR YOUR DOG

You love your Sussex and want to keep him safe. Of course you take every precaution to prevent his escaping from the yard or becoming lost or stolen. You have a sturdy high fence and you always keep your dog on lead when out and about in public places. If your dog is not properly identified, however, you are overlooking a major aspect of his safety. We hope to never be in a situation where our dog is missing, but we should practice prevention in the unfortunate case that this happens; identification greatly increases the chances of your dog's being returned to you.

THE MONTHLY GRIND

If your dog doesn't like the feeling of nail clippers or if you're not comfortable using them, you may wish to try an electric nail grinder. This tool has a small sandpaper disc on the end that rotates to grind the nails down. Some feel that using a grinder reduces the risk of cutting into the quick; this can be true if the tool is used properly. Usually you will be able to tell where the quick is before you get to it. A benefit of the grinder is that it creates a smooth finish on the nails so that there are no ragged edges. Because the tool makes noise, your dog should be introduced to it before the actual grinding takes place. Turn it on and let your dog hear the noise; turn it off and let him inspect it with you holding it. Use the grinder gently, holding it firmly and progressing a little at a time until you reach the proper length. Look at the nail as you grind so that you do not go too short. Stop at any indication that you are nearing the quick. It will take a few sessions for both you and the puppy to get used to the grinder. Make sure that you don't let his hair get tangled in the grinder!

There are several ways to identify your dog. First, the traditional dog tag should be a staple in your dog's wardrobe, attached to his everyday collar. Tags can be made of sturdy plastic and various metals and should include your contact information so that a person who finds the dog can get in touch with you right away to arrange his return. Many people today enjoy the wide range of decorative tags available, so have fun and create a tag to match your dog's personality. Of course, it is important that the tag stays on the collar, so have a secure "O" ring attachment; you also can explore the type of tag that slides right onto the collar.

In addition to the ID tag, which every dog should wear even if identified by another method, two other forms of identification have become popular: microchipping and tattooing. In microchipping, a tiny scannable chip is painlessly inserted under the dog's skin. The number is registered to you so that, if your lost dog turns up at a clinic or shelter, the chip can be scanned to retrieve your contact information.

The advantage of the microchip is that it is a permanent form of ID, but there are some factors to consider. Several different companies make microchips, and not all are compatible with the others' scanning devices. It's best to find a company with a universal microchip that can be read by scanners made by other companies as well. It won't do any good to have the dog chipped if the information cannot be retrieved. Also, not every humane society, shelter and clinic is equipped with a scanner, although more and more facilities are equipping themselves. In fact, many shelters microchip dogs that they adopt out to new homes.

Because the microchip is not visible to the eye, the dog must wear a tag that states that he is microchipped so that whoever picks him up will know to have him scanned. He of course also should have a tag with your contact information in case his chip cannot be read. Humane societies and veterinary clinics offer microchipping service, which is usually very affordable.

Though less popular than microchipping, tattooing is another permanent method of ID for dogs. Most vets perform this service, and there are also clinics that perform dog tattooing. This is also an affordable procedure and one that will not cause much discomfort for the dog. It is best to put the tattoo in a visible area, such as the ear, to deter theft. It is sad to say that there are cases of dogs' being stolen and sold to research laboratories, but such laboratories will not accept tattooed dogs.

To ensure that the tattoo is effective in aiding your dog's return to you, the tattoo number must be registered with a national organization. That way, when someone finds a tattooed dog, a phone call to the registry will quickly match the dog with his owner.

HIT THE ROAD

Car travel with your Sussex may be limited to necessity only, such as trips to the vet, or you may bring your dog along almost everywhere you go. This will depend much on your individual dog and how he reacts to rides in the car. You can begin desensitizing your dog to car travel as a pup so that it's something that he's used to. Still, some dogs suffer from motion sickness. Your vet may prescribe a medication for this if trips in the car pose a problem for your dog. At the very least, you will need to get him to the vet, so he will need to tolerate these trips with the least amount of hassle possible.

Start by taking your pup on short trips, maybe just around the block to start. If he is fine with short trips, lengthen your rides a little at a time. Start to take him on your errands or just for drives around town. By this time it will be easy to tell whether your dog is a born traveler or would prefer staying at home when you are on the road.

Of course, safety is a concern for dogs in the car. First, he must travel securely, not left loose to roam about the car where he could be injured or distract the driver. A young pup can be held by a passenger initially but should soon graduate to a travel crate, which can be the same crate he uses in the home. Other options include a car harness (like a seat belt for dogs) and partitioning the back of the car with a gate made for this purpose.

Bring along what you will need for the dog. He should wear his collar and ID tags, of course, and you should bring his leash, water (and food if a long trip) and clean-up materials for potty breaks and in case of motion sickness. Always keep your dog on his leash when you make stops, and never leave him alone in the car. Many a dog has died from the heat inside a closed car; this does not take much time at all. A dog left alone inside a car can also be a target for thieves.

BOARDING

Today there are many options for dog owners who need someone to care for their dogs in certain circumstances. While many think of boarding their dogs as something to do when away on vacation, many others use the services of doggie "daycare" facilities, dropping their dogs off to spend the day while they are at work. Many of these facilities offer both long-term and daily care. Many go beyond just boarding and cater to all sorts of needs, with on-site grooming, veterinary care, training classes and even "web-cams" where owners can log onto the Internet and check out what their dogs are up to. Most dogs enjoy the activity and time spent with other dogs.

Before you need to use such a service, check out the ones in your

area. Make visits to see the facilities, meet the staff, discuss fees and available services and see whether this is a place where you think your dog will be happy. It is best to do your research in advance so that you're not stuck at the last minute, forced into making a rushed decision without knowing whether the kennel that you've chosen meets your standards. You also can check with your vet's office to see whether they offer boarding for their clients or can recommend a good kennel in the area.

The kennel will need to see proof of your dog's health records and vaccinations so as not to spread illness from dog to dog. Your dog also will need proper identification. Owners usually experience some separation anxiety the first time they have to leave their dog in someone else's care, so it's reassuring to know that the kennel you choose is run by experienced, caring, true dog people.

Visit local boarding kennels to find one that suits your needs and with which you feel comfortable. Perhaps your vet or breeder has boarding facilities or can recommend a suitable kennel.

TRAINING YOUR

SUSSEX SPANIEL

BASIC TRAINING PRINCIPLES: PUPPY VS. ADULT

There's a big difference between training an adult dog and training a young puppy. With a young puppy, everything is new! At eight to ten weeks of age, he will be experiencing many things, and he has nothing with which to compare these experiences. Up to this point, he has been with his dam and littermates, not one-on-one with people except in his interactions with his breeder and visitors to the litter.

When you first bring the puppy home, he is eager to please you. This means that he accepts doing things your way. During the next couple of months, he will absorb the basis of everything he needs to know for the rest of his life. This early age is even referred to as the "sponge" stage. After that, for the next 18 months, it's up to you to reinforce good manners by building on the foundation that you've established. Once your puppy is reliable in basic commands and behavior and has reached the appropriate age, you may gradually introduce him to some of the interesting sports,

games and activities available to pet owners and their dogs.

Raising your puppy is a family affair. Each member of the family must know what rules to set forth for the puppy and how to use the same one-word commands to mean exactly the same thing every time. Even if yours is a large family, one person will soon be considered by the pup to be the leader, the alpha person in his pack, the "boss" who must be obeyed. Often that highly regarded person turns out to be the one who feeds the puppy. Food ranks very high on the puppy's list of important things! That's why your puppy is rewarded with small treats along with verbal praise when he responds to you correctly. As the puppy learns to do what you want him to do, the food rewards are gradually eliminated and only the praise remains. If you were to keep up with the food treats, you could have two problems on your hands—an obese dog and a beggar.

Training begins the minute your Sussex puppy steps through the doorway of your home, so don't make the mistake of putting the puppy on the floor and telling him by your actions to "Go for it! Run wild!" Even if this is your first puppy, you must act as if you know what you're doing: be the boss. An uncertain pup may be terrified to move, while a bold one will be ready to take you at your word and start plotting to destroy the house! Before you collected your puppy, you decided where his own special place would be, and that's where to put him when you first arrive home. Give him a house tour after he has investigated his area and had a nap and a bathroom "pit stop."

It's worth mentioning here that, if you've adopted an adult dog that is completely trained to

your liking, lucky you! You're off the hook! However, if that dog spent his life up to this point in a kennel, or even in a good home but without any real training, be prepared to tackle the job ahead. A dog three years of age or older with no previous training cannot be blamed for not knowing what he was never taught. While the dog is trying to understand and learn your rules, at the same time he has to unlearn many of his previously self-taught habits and general view of the world.

Working with a professional trainer will speed up your progress with an adopted adult dog. You'll need patience, too. Some new

All members of the family should take part in the Sussex Spaniel's training to ensure that the dog will obey no matter who gives the commands.

rules may be close to impossible for the dog to accept. After all, he's been successful so far by doing everything his way! (Patience

THE RIGHT START

The best advice for a potential dog owner is to start with the very best puppy that money can buy. Don't shop around for a bargain in the newspaper. You're buying a companion, not a used car or a second-hand appliance. The purchase price of the dog represents a very significant part of the investment, but this is indeed a very small sum compared to the expenses of maintaining the dog in good health. If you purchase a well-bred, healthy and sound puppy, you will be starting right. An unhealthy puppy can cost you thousands of dollars in unnecessary veterinary expenses and, possibly, a fortune in heartbreak as well.

again.) He may agree with your instruction for a few days and then slip back into his old ways, so you must be just as consistent and understanding in your teaching as you would be with a puppy. (More patience needed yet again!) Your dog has to learn to pay attention to your voice, your family, the daily routine, new smells, new sounds and, in some cases, even a new climate.

One of the most important things to find out about a newly adopted adult dog is his reaction to children (yours and others), strangers and your friends and how he acts upon meeting other dogs. If he was not socialized with dogs as a puppy, this could be a major problem. This does not mean that he's a "bad" dog, a vicious dog or an aggressive dog; rather, it means that he has no idea how to read another dog's body language. There's no way for him to tell whether the other dog is a friend or foe. Survival instinct takes over, telling him to attack first and ask questions later. This definitely calls for professional help and, even then, may not be a behavior that can be corrected 100% reliably (or even at all). If you have a puppy, this is why it is so very important to introduce your young puppy properly to other puppies and "dog-friendly" adult dogs.

Sussex Spaniels taught systematically and fairly have no

predilection for difficulty with any command. Systematic and fair education that lays a good base upon which all other training is built is essential. The Sussex Spaniel will not react well to harsh training, but he will respond favorably to gentle motivational methods and sincere praise and encouragement. The reinforcement of praise from his owner and the approval that praise conveys are of utmost importance as befits his loyalty to his owner. Now let us get started.

HOUSE-TRAINING YOUR SUSSEX

Dogs are tactility-oriented when it comes to house-training. In other words, they respond to the surface on which they are given approval to eliminate. The choice is yours (the dog's version is in parentheses): The lawn (including the neighbors' lawns)? A bare patch of earth under a tree (where people like to sit and relax in the summertime)? Concrete steps or patio (all sidewalks, garages and basement floors)? The curbside (watch out for cars)? A small area of crushed stone in a corner of the yard (mine!)? The latter is the best choice if you can manage it, because it will remain strictly for the dog's use and is easy to keep clean.

You can start out with paper-training indoors and switch over to an outdoor surface as the puppy matures and gains control over his need to eliminate. For the nay-sayers, don't worry—this won't mean that the dog will soil on every piece of newspaper lying around the house. You are training him to go outside, remember?

Accustom your pup to his lead and collar and start taking him to his relief area right away. Your pup can't tell you when it's time "to go," so it's best to err on the side of caution.

CANINE DEVELOPMENT SCHEDULE

It is important to understand how and at what age a puppy develops into adulthood.
If you are a puppy owner, consult this Canine Development Schedule to
determine the stage of development your puppy is currently experiencing.
This knowledge will help you as you work with the puppy in the weeks and months ahead.

PERIOD	AGE	CHARACTERISTICS
FIRST TO THIRD	BIRTH TO SEVEN WEEKS	Puppy needs food, sleep and warmth and responds to simple and gentle touching. Needs mother for security and disciplining. Needs littermates for learning and interacting with other dogs. Pup learns to function within a pack and learns pack order of dominance. Begin socializing pup with adults and children for short periods. Pup begins to become aware of his environment.
FOURTH	EIGHT TO TWELVE WEEKS	Brain is fully developed. Pup needs socializing with outside world. Remove from mother and littermates. Needs to change from canine pack to human pack. Human dominance necessary. Fear period occurs between 8 and 10 weeks. Avoid fright and pain.
FIFTH	THIRTEEN TO SIXTEEN WEEKS	Training and formal obedience should begin. Less association with other dogs, more with people, places, situations. Period will pass easily if you remember this is pup's change-to-adolescence time. Be firm and fair. Flight instinct prominent. Permissiveness and over-disciplining can do permanent damage. Praise for good behavior.
JUVENILE	FOUR TO EIGHT MONTHS	Another fear period about seven to eight months of age. It passes quickly, but be cautious of fright and pain. Sexual maturity reached. Dominant traits established. Dog should understand sit, down, come and stay by now.

NOTE: THESE ARE APPROXIMATE TIME FRAMES. ALLOW FOR INDIVIDUAL DIFFERENCES IN PUPPIES.

Starting out by paper-training often is the only choice for a city dog.

WHEN YOUR PUPPY'S "GOT TO GO"

Your puppy's need to relieve himself is seemingly non-stop, but signs of improvement will be seen each week. From 8 to 10 weeks old, the puppy will have to be taken outside every time he wakes up, about 10 to 15 minutes after every meal and after every period of play—all day long, from first thing in the morning until his bedtime! That's a total of ten or more trips per day to teach the puppy where it's okay to relieve himself. With that schedule in mind, you can see that house-training a young puppy is not a part-time job. It requires someone to be home all day.

If that seems overwhelming or impossible, do a little planning. For example, plan to pick up your puppy at the start of a vacation period. If you can't get home in the middle of the day, plan to hire a dog-sitter or ask a neighbor to

> **OUR CANINE KIDS**
> "Everything I learned about parenting, I learned from my dog." How often adults recognize that their parenting skills are mere extensions of the education they acquired while caring for their dogs. Many owners refer to their dogs as their "kids" and treat their canine companions like real members of the family. Surveys indicate that a majority of dog owners talk to their dogs regularly, celebrate their dogs' birthdays and purchase Christmas gifts for their dogs. Another survey shows that dog owners take their dogs to the veterinarian more frequently than they visit their own physicians.

"Can't he see that the bathroom is occupied?"

late on the job. Remind yourself—repeatedly—that this hectic schedule improves as the puppy gets older.

HOME WITHIN A HOME

Your Sussex puppy needs to be confined to one secure, puppy-proof area when no one is able to watch his every move. Generally, the kitchen is the place of choice because the floor is washable. Likewise, it's a busy family area that will accustom the pup to a variety of noises, everything from pots and pans to the telephone, blender and dishwasher. He will also be enchanted by the smell of your cooking (and will never be critical when you burn something). An exercise pen (also called an "ex-pen," a puppy version of a playpen) with high sides so that the pup cannot climb out can help to confine a young pup. He can see out and has a certain amount of space in which to run about, but he is safe from dangerous things like electrical cords, heating units, trash baskets or open kitchen-supply cabinets. Place the pen where the puppy will not get a blast of heat or air conditioning.

In the pen, you can put a few toys, his bed (which can be his crate if the dimensions of pen and crate are compatible) and a few layers of newspaper in one small corner, just in case. A water bowl can be hung at a convenient

POTTY COMMAND

Most dogs love to please their masters; there are no bounds to what dogs will do to make their owners happy. The potty command is a good example of this theory. If toileting on command makes the master happy, then more power to him. Puppies will obligingly piddle if it really makes their keepers smile. Some owners can be creative about which word they will use to command their dogs to relieve themselves. Some popular choices are "Potty," "Tinkle," "Piddle," "Let's go," "Hurry up" and "Toilet." Give the command every time your puppy goes into position and the puppy will begin to associate his business with the command.

come over to take the pup outside, feed him his lunch and then take him out again about ten or so minutes after he's eaten. Also make arrangements with that or another person to be your "emergency" contact if you have to stay height on the side of the ex-pen so it won't become a splashing pool for an innovative puppy. His food dish can go on the floor, next to but not under the water bowl.

Crates are something that pet owners are at last getting used to for their dogs. Wild or domestic canines have always preferred to sleep in den-like safe spots, and that is exactly what the crate provides. How often have you seen adult dogs that choose to sleep under a table or chair even though they have full run of the house? It's the den connection.

In your "happy" voice, use the word "Crate" every time you put the pup into his den. If he's new to a crate, toss in a small biscuit for him to chase the first few times. At night, after he's been outside, he should sleep in his crate. The crate may be kept in his designated area at night or, if you want to be sure to hear those wake-up yips in the morning, put the crate in a corner of your bedroom. However, don't make any response whatsoever to whining or crying. If he's completely ignored, he'll settle down and get to sleep.

Good bedding for a young puppy is an old folded bath towel or an old blanket, something that is easily washable and disposable if necessary ("accidents" will happen!). Never put newspaper in the puppy's crate. Also those old ideas about adding a clock to

DAILY SCHEDULE

How many relief trips does your puppy need per day? A puppy up to the age of 14 weeks will need to go outside about 8 to 12 times per day! You will have to take the pup out any time he starts sniffing around the floor or turning in small circles, as well as after naps, meals, games and lessons or whenever he's released from his crate. Once the puppy is 14 to 22 weeks of age, he will require only 6 to 8 relief trips. At the ages of 22 to 32 weeks, the puppy will require about 5 to 7 trips. Adult dogs typically require 4 relief trips per day, in the morning, afternoon, evening and late at night.

replace his mother's heartbeat or a hot-water bottle to replace her warmth are just that—old ideas. The clock could drive the puppy nuts, and the hot-water bottle could end up as a very soggy waterbed! An extremely good breeder would have introduced your puppy to the crate by letting two pups sleep together for a couple of nights, followed by several nights alone. How thankful you will be if you found that breeder!

Safe toys in the pup's crate or area will keep him occupied, but monitor their condition closely. Discard any toys that show signs of being chewed to bits. Squeaky

parts, bits of stuffing or plastic or any other small pieces can cause intestinal blockage or possibly choking if ingested.

PROGRESSING WITH POTTY-TRAINING
After you've taken your puppy out and he has relieved himself in the area you've selected, he can have some free time with the family as long as there is someone responsible for watching him. That doesn't mean just someone in the same room who is watching TV or busy on the computer, but one person who is doing nothing other than keeping an eye on the pup, playing with him on the floor and helping him understand his position in the pack.

This first taste of freedom will let you begin to set the house rules. If you don't want the dog on the furniture, now is the time to prevent his first attempts to jump up onto the couch. The word to use in this case is "Off," not "Down." "Down" is the word you will use to teach the down position, which is something entirely different.

Most corrections at this stage come in the form of simply distracting the puppy. Instead of telling him "No" for "Don't chew the carpet," distract the chomping puppy with a toy and he'll forget about the carpet.

As you are playing with the pup, do not forget to watch him closely and pay attention to his

TIDY BOY

Clean by nature, dogs do not like to soil their dens, which in effect are their crates or sleeping quarters. Unless not feeling well, dogs will not defecate or urinate in their crates. Crate training capitalizes on the dog's natural desire to keep his den clean. Be conscientious about giving the puppy as many opportunities to relieve himself outdoors as possible. Reward the puppy for correct behavior. Praise him and pat him whenever he "goes" in the correct location. Even the tidiest of puppies can have potty accidents, so be patient and dedicate more energy to helping your puppy achieve a clean lifestyle.

body language. Whenever you see him begin to circle or sniff, take the puppy outside to relieve himself. If you are paper-training, put him back into his confined area on the newspapers. In either case, praise him as he eliminates while he actually is in the act of relieving himself. Three seconds after he has finished is too late. You'll be praising him for running toward you, picking up a toy or whatever he may be doing at that moment, and that's not what you want to be praising him for. Timing is a vital tool in all dog training. Use it!

Remove soiled newspapers immediately and replace them with clean ones. You may want to take a small piece of soiled paper and place it in the middle of the new clean papers, as the scent will attract him to that spot when it's time to go again. That scent attraction is why it's so important to clean up any messes made in the house by using a product specially made to eliminate the odor of dog urine and droppings. Regular household cleansers won't do the trick. Pet shops sell the best pet deodorizers. Invest in the largest container you can find.

Scent attraction eventually will lead your pup to his chosen spot outdoors; this is the basis of outdoor training. When you take your puppy outside to relieve himself, use a one-word command such as "Outside" or "Go-potty"

EXTRA! EXTRA!
The headlines read: "Puppy Piddles Here!" Breeders commonly use newspapers to line their whelping pens, so puppies learn to associate newspapers with relieving themselves. Do not use newspapers to line your pup's crate, as this will signal to your puppy that it is OK to urinate in his crate. If you choose to paper-train your puppy, you will layer newspapers on a section of the floor near the door he uses to go outside. You should encourage the puppy to use the papers to relieve himself, and bring him there whenever you see him getting ready to go. Little by little, you will reduce the size of the newspaper-covered area so that the puppy will learn to relieve himself "on the other side of the door."

(that's one word to the puppy!) as you attach his leash. Then lead him to his spot. Now comes the hard part—hard for you, that is. Just stand there until he urinates and defecates. Move him a few feet in one direction or another if he's just sitting there looking at you, but remember that this is neither playtime nor time for a walk. This is strictly a business trip! Then, as he circles and squats (remember your timing!), give him a quiet "Good dog" as praise. If you start to jump for joy, ecstatic over his performance, he'll do one of two things: either he will stop mid-stream, as it were, or he'll do it again for you—in the house—and expect you to be just as delighted!

Give him five minutes or so and, if he doesn't go in that time, take him back indoors to his confined area and try again in another ten minutes or immediately if you see him sniffing and circling. By careful observation, you'll soon work out a successful schedule.

Accidents, by the way, are just that—accidents. Clean them up quickly and thoroughly, without comment, after the puppy has been taken outside to finish his business and then put back into his area or crate. If you witness an accident in progress, say "No!" in a stern voice and get the pup outdoors immediately. No punishment is needed. You and your puppy are just learning each other's language, and sometimes it's easy to miss a puppy's message. Chalk it up to experience and watch more closely from now on.

KEEPING THE PACK ORDERLY
Discipline is a form of training that brings order to life. For example, military discipline is what allows the soldiers in an army to work as one. Discipline is a form of teaching and, in dogs, is the basis of how the successful pack operates. Each member knows his place in the pack and all respect the leader, or alpha dog. It is essential for your puppy that you establish this type of relationship, with you as the alpha, or leader. It is a form of social coexistence that all canines recognize and accept. Discipline, therefore, is never to be confused with punishment. When you teach your puppy how you want him to behave, and he behaves properly and you praise him for it, you are disciplining him with a form of positive reinforcement.

For a dog, rewards come in the form of praise, a smile, a cheerful tone of voice, a few friendly pats or a rub of the ears. Rewards are also small food treats. Obviously, that does not mean bits of regular dog food. Instead, treats are very small bits of special things like cheese or pieces of soft dog treats. The idea is to reward the dog with something very small that he can taste and swallow, providing instant positive reinforcement. If he has to take time to chew the treat, he will have forgotten what he did to earn it by the time he is finished.

Your puppy should never be physically punished. The displeasure shown on your face and in your voice is sufficient to signal to the pup that he has done something wrong. He wants to please everyone higher up on the social ladder, especially his leader, so a scowl and harsh voice will take care of the error. Growling out the word "Shame!" when the pup is caught in the act of doing something wrong is better than the repetitive "No." Some dogs hear "No" so often that they begin to think it's their name! By the way, do not use the dog's name when you're correcting him. His name is reserved to get his attention for something pleasant about to take place.

There are punishments that have nothing to do with you. For example, your dog may think that chasing cats is one reason for his existence. You can try to stop it as much as you like but without success, because it's such fun for the dog. But one good hissing, spitting swipe of a cat's claws across the dog's nose will put an end to the game forever. Intervene only when your dog's eyeball is seriously at risk. Cat scratches can cause permanent damage to an innocent but annoying puppy.

PUPPY KINDERGARTEN

COLLAR AND LEASH
Before you begin your Sussex puppy's education, he must be used to his collar and leash. Choose a collar for your puppy that is secure but not heavy or bulky. He won't enjoy training if he's uncomfortable. A flat buckle collar is fine for everyday wear

and for initial puppy training. For older dogs, there are several types of training collars such as the martingale, which is a double loop that tightens slightly around the neck, or the head collar, which is similar to a horse's halter. Do not use a chain choke collar with your Sussex Spaniel. This is a breed that thrives on positive training methods, not constant or harsh correction.

A lightweight 6-foot woven cotton or nylon training leash is preferred by most trainers because it is easy to fold up in your hand and comfortable to hold because there is a certain amount of give to it. There are

Sussex Spaniels appreciate praise more than any treat, but a treat can be a helpful motivator as long as you never forget the petting and words of encouragement.

lessons where the dog will start off 6 feet away from you at the end of the leash. The leash used to take the puppy outside to relieve himself is shorter because you don't want him to roam away from his area. The shorter leash will also be the one to use when you walk the puppy.

If you've been wise enough to enroll in a puppy kindergarten training class, suggestions will be made as to the best collar and leash for your young puppy. I say "wise" because your puppy will be in a class with puppies in his age range (up to five months old) of all breeds and sizes. It's the perfect way for him to learn the right way (and the wrong way) to interact with other dogs as well as their people. You cannot teach your puppy how to interpret another dog's sign language. For a first-time puppy owner, these socialization classes are invaluable. For experienced dog owners, they are a real boon to further training.

Conduct training sessions with your Sussex in a securely enclosed location, because if he should be distracted by something that he deems more interesting, he'll be off and running in no time.

KEEP IT SIMPLE—AND FUN

Keep your lessons simple, interesting and user-friendly. Fun breaks help you both. Spend two minutes or ten teaching your puppy, but practice only as long as your dog enjoys what he's doing and is focused on pleasing you. If he's bored or distracted, stop the training session after any correct response (always end on a high note!). After a few minutes of playtime, you can go back to "hitting the books."

ATTENTION AND REWARDS

You've been using the dog's name since the minute you collected him from the breeder, so you should be able to get his attention by saying his name—with a big smile and in an excited tone of voice. His response will be the puppy equivalent of "Here I am! What are we going to do?" Your immediate response (if you haven't guessed by now) is "Good dog." Rewarding him at the moment he pays attention to you teaches him the proper way to respond when he hears his name. The Sussex Spaniel is not as food-motivated as many breeds; he relishes praise from his owner much more. However, tidbits can be helpful in getting the dog's attention and teaching new exercises, as long as you don't skimp on the praise!

You will not use food forever in training. Food is only used to teach new behaviors and, once the dog knows what you want when you give a specific command, you will wean him off the food treats but still maintain the verbal praise, which the Sussex appreciates more than a biscuit or sliver of liver.

In general, training the Sussex Spaniel must be fun for owner and dog. The Sussex is always up to a game. Care must be taken to avoid any type of training routines that are overly repetitious and boring; the intelligence of the breed demands this.

DON'T STRESS ME OUT

Your dog doesn't have to deal with paying the bills, the daily commute, PTA meetings and the like, but, believe it or not, there's a lot of stress in a dog's world. Stress can be caused by the owner's impatient demeanor and his angry or harsh corrections. If your dog cringes when you reach for his training collar, he's stressed. An older dog is sometimes stressed out when he goes to a new home. No matter what the cause, put off all training until he's over it. If he's going through a fear period—shying away from people, trembling when spoken to, avoiding eye contact or hiding under furniture—wait to resume training. Naturally you'd also postpone your lessons if the dog were sick, and the same goes for you. Show some compassion.

While seemingly "unable" to hear a command at will, the Sussex often chooses when to respond. As such, much praise and positive reinforcement are necessary, as the Sussex responds to these above all else in training.

Training your Sussex Spaniel to sit upon command is a necessary exercise and one that can be achieved quite easily.

EXERCISES FOR A BASIC CANINE EDUCATION

THE SIT EXERCISE

There are several ways to teach the puppy to sit. The first one is to catch him whenever he is about to sit and, as his backside nears the floor, say "Sit, good dog!"

LEADER OF THE PACK

Canines are pack animals. They live according to pack rules, and every pack has only one leader. Guess what? That's you! To establish your position of authority, lay down the rules and be fair and good-natured in all your dealings with your dog. He will consider young children as his littermates, but the one who trains him, who feeds him, who grooms him, who expects him to come into line, that's his leader. And he who leads must be obeyed.

his nose goes up in the air and his head tilts back as he follows the treat in your hand. At that point, he will have to either sit or fall over, so as his back legs buckle under, say "Sit, good dog," and then give him the treat and lots of praise. You may have to begin with your hand lightly running up his chest, actually lifting his chin up until he sits. Some (usually older) dogs require gentle pressure on their hindquarters with the left hand, in which case the dog should be on your left side. Puppies generally do not appreciate this physical dominance.

That's positive reinforcement and, if your timing is sharp, he will learn that what he's doing at that second is connected to your saying "Sit" and that you think he's clever for doing it!

Another method is to start with the puppy on his leash in front of you. Show him a treat in the palm of your right hand. Bring your hand up under his nose and, almost in slow motion, move your hand up and back so

After a few times, you should be able to show the dog a treat in the open palm of your hand, raise your hand waist-high as you say "Sit" and have him sit. You will thereby have taught him two things at the same time. Both the verbal command and the motion of the hand are signals for the sit. Your puppy is watching you almost more than he is listening to you, so what you do is just as important as what you say.

Don't save any of these drills only for training sessions. Use them as much as possible at odd times during a normal day. The dog should always sit before being given his food dish. He should sit to let you go through a doorway first, when the doorbell rings or when you stop to speak to someone on the street.

Remember to always praise enthusiastically, because Sussex Spaniels relish verbal praise from their owners and feel so proud of themselves whenever they accomplish a behavior.

THE DOWN EXERCISE

Before beginning to teach the down command, you must consider how the dog feels about this exercise. To him, "down" is a submissive position. Being flat on the floor with you standing over him is not his idea of fun. It's up to you to let him know that, while it may not be fun, the reward of your approval is worth his effort.

Start with the puppy on your left side in a sit position. Hold the leash right above his collar in your left hand. Have an extra-special treat, such as a small piece of cooked chicken or hot dog, in your right hand. Place it at the end of the pup's nose and steadily move your hand down and forward along the ground. Hold the leash to prevent a sudden lunge for the food. As the puppy goes into the down position, say "Down" very gently.

The difficulty with this exercise is twofold: it's both the submissive aspect and the fact that most people say the word "Down" as if they were drill sergeants in charge of recruits! So issue the command sweetly, give him the treat and have the pup

maintain the down position for several seconds. If he tries to get up immediately, place your hands on his shoulders and press down gently, giving him a very quiet "Good dog." As you progress with this lesson, increase the "down time" until he will hold it until you say "Okay" (his cue for release). Practice this one in the

DOWN

"Down" is a harsh-sounding word and a submissive posture in dog body language, thus presenting two obstacles in teaching the down command. When the dog is about to flop down on his own, tell him "Good down." Pups that are not good about being handled learn better by having food lowered in front of them. A dog that trusts you can be gently guided into position. When you give the command "Down," be sure to say it sweetly!

One of the biggest challenges in training is keeping the student focused and attentive. Teaching a lesson is pointless if the dog becomes bored by repetition or if his attention is elsewhere.

house at various times throughout the day.

By increasing the length of time during which the dog must maintain the down position, you'll find many uses for it. For example, he can lie at your feet in the vet's office or anywhere that both of you have to wait, when you are on the phone, while the family is eating and so forth. If you progress to training for competitive obedience, he'll already be all set for the exercise called the "long down."

THE STAY EXERCISE

You can teach your Sussex to stay in the sit, down and stand positions. To teach the sit/stay, have the dog sit on your left side. Hold the leash at waist level in your left hand and let the dog know that you have a treat in your closed right hand. Step forward on your right foot as you say "Stay." Immediately turn and stand directly in front of the dog, keeping your right hand up high so he'll keep his eye on the treat hand and maintain the sit position for a count of five. Return to your original position and offer the reward.

Increase the length of the sit/stay each time until the dog can hold it for at least 30 seconds without moving. After about a week of success, move out on your right foot and take two steps before turning to face the dog. Give the "Stay" hand signal (left palm back toward the dog's head) as you leave. He gets the treat when you return and he holds the sit/stay. Increase the distance that you walk away from him before turning until you reach the length of your training leash. But don't rush it. Go back to the beginning if he moves before he should. No matter what the lesson, never be upset by having to back up for a few days. The repetition and practice are what will make your dog reliable in these commands. It won't do any good to move on to something more difficult if the command is not mastered at the easier levels. Above all, even if you do get frustrated, never let your puppy know. Always keep a positive, upbeat attitude during training, which will transmit to your dog for positive results.

The down/stay is taught in the same way once the dog is completely reliable and steady with the down command. Again, don't rush it. With the dog in the down position on your left side, step out on your right foot as you say "Stay." Return by walking around in back of the dog and into your original position. While you are training, it's okay to murmur something like "Hold on" to encourage him to stay put. When the dog will stay without moving when you are at a distance of 3 or 4 feet, begin to increase the length of time before you return. Be sure he holds the down on your return until you say "Okay." At that point, he gets his treat—just so he'll remember for next time that it's not over until it's over.

CREATURES OF HABIT

Canine behaviorists and trainers aptly describe dogs as "creatures of habit," meaning that dogs respond to structure in their daily lives and welcome a routine. Do not interpret this to mean that dogs enjoy endless repetition in their training sessions. Dogs get bored just as humans do. Keep training sessions interesting and exciting. Vary the commands and the locations in which you practice. Give short breaks for play in between lessons. A bored student will never be the best performer in the class.

THE COME EXERCISE

Since the Sussex has the tendency to respond to a command when he chooses, it is essential that a puppy be taught a reliable recall, or "come," command. Training the Sussex Spaniel to come when called as a reflex behavior is essential and best taught as a puppy. It is for the good of the dog that a reliable recall is so important; a dog that does not reliably come when called cannot be called out of danger.

Therefore no command is more important to the safety of your Sussex than "Come." It is what you should say every single time you see the puppy running toward you: "Percy, come! Good dog." During playtime, run a few feet away from the puppy and turn and tell him to "Come" as he is already running to you. You can go so far as to teach your puppy two things at once if you squat down and hold out your arms. As the pup gets close to you and

You'll know that you've achieved success with the come command when your Sussex runs to you this enthusiastically!

you're saying "Good dog," bring your right arm in about waist high. Now he's also learning the hand signal, an excellent device should you be on the phone when you need to get him to come to you. You'll also both be one step ahead when you enter obedience classes.

When the puppy responds to your well-timed "Come," try it with the puppy on the training leash. This time, catch him off-guard, while he's sniffing a leaf or watching a bird: "Percy, come!" You may have to pause for a split second after his name to be sure you have his attention. If the puppy shows any sign of confusion, give the leash a mild jerk and take a couple of steps backward. Do not repeat the command. In this case, you should say "Good come" as he reaches you.

That's an essential rule of training. Each command word is given just once. Anything more is nagging. You'll also notice that all commands are one word only. Even when they are actually two words, you say them as one.

Never call the dog to come to you—with or without his name—if you are angry or intend to correct him for some misbehavior. When correcting the pup, you go to him. Your dog must always connect "Come" with something pleasant and with your approval; then you can rely on his response.

Puppies, like children, have notoriously short attention spans, so don't overdo it with any of the training. Keep each lesson short. Break it up with a quick run around the yard or a ball toss, repeat the lesson and quit as soon as the pup gets it right. That way, you will always end with a "Good dog."

Life isn't perfect and neither are puppies. A time will come, often around ten months of age, when he'll become "selectively deaf" or choose to "forget" his name. He may respond by wagging his tail (and even seeming to smile at you) with a look that says "Make me!" Laugh, throw his favorite toy and skip the lesson you had planned. Pups will be pups!

THE HEEL EXERCISE

The second most important command to teach, after the come, is the heel. When you are walking your growing puppy, you need to be in control. Besides, it looks terrible to be pulled and yanked down the street, and it's not much fun either. Your eight- to ten-week-old puppy will probably follow you everywhere, but that's his natural instinct, not your control over the situation. However, any time he does follow you, you can say "Heel" and be ahead of the game, as he will learn to associate this command with the action of following you before you even begin teaching him to heel.

There is a very precise, almost

Make eye contact with your dog as you train him to heel and let him know what is expected of him.

With patience and practice, your Sussex will soon be right in step with you, at your pace.

The show dog takes the heel command a step further, as he must heel beside his handler in the ring while the judge evaluates his movement.

military, procedure for teaching your dog to heel. As with all other obedience training, begin with the dog on your left side. He will be in a very nice sit and you will have the training leash across your chest. Hold the loop and folded leash in your right hand. Pick up the slack leash above the dog in your left hand and hold it loosely at your side. Step out on your left foot as you say "Heel." If the puppy does not move, give a gentle tug or pat your left leg to get him started. If he surges ahead of you, stop and pull him back gently until he is at your side. Tell him to sit and begin again.

Walk a few steps and stop while the puppy is correctly beside you. Tell him to sit and give mild verbal praise. (More enthusiastic praise will encourage him to think the lesson is over.) Repeat the lesson, increasing the number of steps you take only as long as the dog is heeling nicely beside you. When you end the lesson, have him hold the sit, then give him the "Okay" to let him know that this is the end of the lesson. Praise him so that he knows he did a good job.

The cure for excessive pulling (a common problem) is to stop when the dog is no more than 2 or 3 feet ahead of you. Guide him back into position and begin again. With a really determined puller, try switching to a head collar. When used properly, this will automatically turn the pup's head toward

you so you can bring him back easily to the heel position. Give quiet, reassuring praise every time the leash goes slack and he's staying with you.

Staying and heeling can take a lot out of a dog, so provide playtime and free-running exercise to shake off the stress when the lessons are over. You don't want him to associate training with all work and no fun.

TAPERING OFF TIDBITS
Although praise is the most important motivator with the Sussex Spaniel, you will likely also use food in training new behaviors. Your dog has been watching you—and the hand that treats—throughout all of his lessons, and now it's time to break the treat habit. Begin by giving him treats at the end of each lesson only. Then start to give a treat after the end of only some of

LET'S GO!
Many people use "Let's go" instead of "Heel" when teaching their dogs to behave on lead. It sounds more like fun! When beginning to teach the heel, whatever command you use, always step off on your left foot. That's the one next to the dog, who is on your left side, in case you've forgotten. Keep a loose leash. When the dog pulls ahead, stop, bring him back and begin again. Use treats to guide him around turns.

SHOULD WE ENROLL?
If you have the means and the time, you should definitely take your dog to obedience classes. Begin with Puppy Kindergarten Classes in which puppies of all sizes learn basic lessons while getting the opportunity to meet and greet each other; it's as much about socialization as it is about good manners. What you learn in class you can practice at home. And if you goof up in practice, you'll get help in the next session.

the lessons. At the end of every lesson, as well as during the lessons, be consistent with the praise. Your pup now doesn't know whether he'll get a treat or not, but he should keep performing well just in case. Finally, you will stop giving treat rewards entirely. Save them for something brand-new that you want to teach him. Keep up the praise and you'll always have a "good dog."

OBEDIENCE CLASSES

The advantages of an obedience class are that your dog will have to learn amid the distractions of other people and dogs and that your mistakes will be quickly corrected by the trainer. Teaching your dog along with a qualified instructor and other handlers who may have more dog experience than you is another plus of the class environment. The instructor and other handlers can help you to find the most efficient way of teaching your dog a command or exercise. It's often easier to learn by other people's mistakes than your own.

You will also learn all of the requirements for competitive obedience trials, in which you can earn titles and go on to advanced jumping and retrieving exercises, which are fun for many dogs. Jumping may be difficult for the Sussex, with his short legs and massive body. Extreme care must be taken to avoid stress on the dog's developing skeletal structure. Jumping must be taught systematically and with care to assure good form and to prevent avoidable injury, beginning with very low jump heights and progressing to any required higher heights slowly. Training of this type should not begin until the dog is at least a year old.

While the Sussex is capable of advanced obedience work, and has enjoyed considerable success in the United States, caution is necessary. The prospective owner who wishes to have a competition dog for advanced obedience may do well to reconsider their motives in acquiring a Sussex Spaniel. Obedience classes, however, also build the foundation needed for many other canine activities (in which we humans are allowed to participate, too!).

TRAINING FOR OTHER ACTIVITIES

Once your dog has basic obedience under his collar and is 12 months of age, you can enter the world of agility training. Dogs think agility is pure fun, like being turned loose in an amusement park full of obstacles!

Again, the jumping exercises may be difficult for the Sussex Spaniel and should only be undertaken with extreme caution. The AKC requires the dog to be at least 12 months of age before participating in agility; some organizations require a dog to be 18 months old. The breed is very capable of success in agility competition but,

again, an owner who is choosing a dog first and foremost for agility may do well to consider a breed other than the Sussex Spaniel.

In addition to agility, there are hunting activities for sporting dogs, lure-coursing events for sighthounds, go-to-ground events for terriers, racing for the Nordic sled dogs, herding trials for the shepherd breeds and tracking, which is open to all "nosey" dogs (which would include all dogs!). Sussex Spaniels excel in tracking. The large nose of the Sussex is ideally suited and able to work in a variety of situations that capitalize on his purposeful and powerful scenting ability. Sussex Spaniels have been trained to use their noses in search-and-rescue work, narcotics detection and other similar endeavors in addition to being trained for participation in standard tracking tests.

As a member of the Sporting Group, the Sussex Spaniel is well-suited for hunting game as appropriate to the breed's size. Sussex often are used to locate and flush upland game birds, later retrieving the shot game for the handler back from land or water. Fanciers have also reported success in using Sussex Spaniels on rabbit. They are are typically tenacious and thorough in working cover. Retrieving ability varies among individuals of the breed, with some being quite natural and

If you're interested in obedience competition, start with the basics and progress from there. Obedience exercises build on commands like the sit/stay, requiring extended periods of time, longer distances from the handler and responses to hand signals.

others quite hopeless. Said to be relatively easy to train for the field, care must be taken not to overdo it when training the retrieve. Repetition after repetition will quickly sour a Sussex for the game. While a Sussex, like any other spaniel, may charge out of gun range, a major advantage of the Sussex afield is the breed's tendency to work close.

A number of Sussex Spaniels actively participate as therapy dogs, ranging from specially trained dogs who visit nursing homes and other group-care centers to dogs who actively provide assistance. In functioning as an assistance dog, regard must be given to the overall size of the Sussex Spaniel. For example, a Sussex is not going to make a suitable guide dog for the blind due to his more compact size, but he will do well as a hearing dog. The breed's natural affinity for humans, desire to please and problem-solving ability make the Sussex well suited to this sort of training.

Sussex Spaniels enjoy doing activities with their owners. A trained Sussex Spaniel is a joy to live with, as training and activity provide appropriate outlets for the breed's considerable ability to learn and solve problems. Around the house, your Sussex can be taught to do some simple chores. You might teach him to carry small household items or to fetch the morning newspaper. The kids can teach the dog all kinds of tricks, from playing hide-and-seek to balancing a biscuit on his nose. A family dog is what rounds out the family. Everything he does, including cuddling by your side and gazing lovingly at you, represents the bonus of owning a dog.

RIGHT CLICK ON YOUR DOG

With three clicks, the dolphin jumps through the hoop. Wouldn't it be nice to have a dog who could obey wordless commands that easily? Clicker training actually was developed by dolphin trainers and today is used on dogs with great success. You can buy a clicker at a pet shop or pet-supply outlet, and then you'll be off and clicking.

You can click your dog into learning new commands, shaping or conditioning his behavior and solving bad habits. The clicker, used in conjunction with a treat, is an extension of positive reinforcement. The dog begins to recognize your happy clicking, and will be happy to obey your command. The dog is conditioned to follow your hand with the clicker, just as he would follow your hand with a treat. To discourage the dog from inappropriate behavior (like jumping up or barking), you can use the clicker to set a time frame and then click and reward the dog once he's waited the allotted time without jumping up or barking.

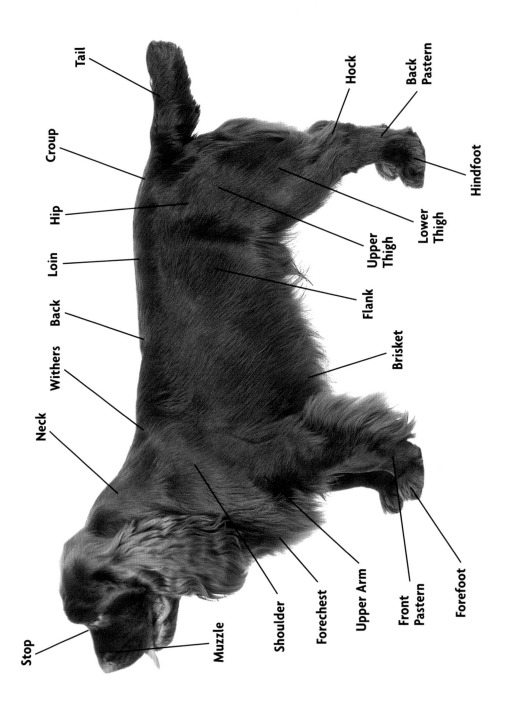

Tail

Croup

Hip

Loin

Back

Withers

Neck

Stop

Muzzle

Shoulder

Forechest

Upper Arm

Front Pastern

Forefoot

Brisket

Flank

Upper Thigh

Lower Thigh

Hindfoot

Back Pastern

Hock

PHYSICAL STRUCTURE OF THE SUSSEX SPANIEL

SUSSEX SPANIEL

BY LOWELL ACKERMAN DVM, DACVD

HEALTHCARE FOR A LIFETIME

When you own a dog, you become his healthcare advocate over his entire lifespan, as well as being the one to shoulder the financial burden of such care. Accordingly, it is worthwhile to focus on prevention rather than treatment, as you and your pet will both be happier.

Of course, the best place to have begun your program of preventive healthcare is with the initial purchase or adoption of your dog. There is no way of guaranteeing that your new furry friend is free of medical problems, but there are some things you can do to improve your odds. You certainly should have done adequate research into the Sussex Spaniel and have selected your puppy carefully rather than buying on impulse. Health issues aside, a large number of pet abandonment and relinquishment cases arise from a mismatch between pet needs and owner expectations. This is entirely preventable with appropriate planning and finding a good breeder.

Regarding healthcare issues specifically, it is very difficult to make blanket statements about where to acquire a problem-free pet, but, again, a reputable breeder is your best bet. In an ideal situation you have the opportunity to see both parents, get references from other owners of the breeder's pups and see genetic-testing documentation for several generations of the litter's ancestors. At the very least, you must thoroughly investigate the Sussex and the problems inherent in that breed, as well as the genetic testing available to screen for those problems. Genetic testing offers some important benefits but is available for only a few disorders in a relatively small number of breeds and is not available for some of the most common genetic diseases, such as hip dysplasia, cataracts, epilepsy, cardiomyopathy, etc. This area of research is indeed exciting and increasingly important, and advances will continue to be made each year. In fact, recent research has shown that there is an equivalent dog gene for 75% of known human genes, so research done in either species is likely to benefit the other.

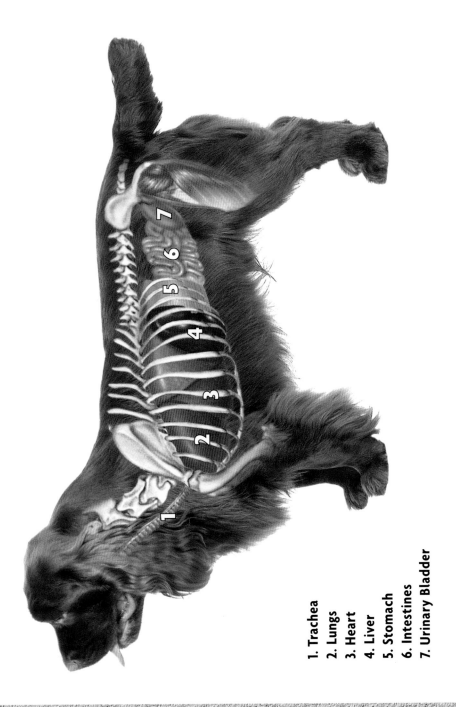

1. Trachea
2. Lungs
3. Heart
4. Liver
5. Stomach
6. Intestines
7. Urinary Bladder

INTERNAL ORGANS OF THE SUSSEX SPANIEL

We've also discussed that evaluating the behavioral nature of your Sussex and that of his immediate family members is an important part of the selection process that cannot be overemphasized. It is sometimes difficult to evaluate temperament in puppies because certain behavioral tendencies, such as some forms of aggression, may not be immediately evident. More dogs are euthanized each year for behavioral reasons than for all medical conditions combined, so it is critical to take temperament issues seriously. Start with a well-balanced, friendly companion and put the time and effort into proper socialization, and you will both be rewarded with a valued relationship.

Assuming that you have started off with a pup from healthy, sound stock, you then become responsible for helping your veterinarian keep your pet healthy. Some crucial things happen before you even bring your puppy home. Parasite control typically begins at two weeks of age, and vaccinations typically begin at six to eight weeks of age. A pre-pubertal evaluation is typically scheduled for about six months of age. At this time, a dental evaluation is done (since the adult teeth are now in), heartworm prevention is started and neutering or spaying is most commonly done.

It is critical to commence regular dental care at home if you have not already done so. It may

YOUR DOG NEEDS TO VISIT THE VET IF:

- He has ingested a toxin such as antifreeze or a toxic plant; in these cases, administer first aid and call the vet right away
- His teeth are discolored, loose or missing or he has sores or other signs of infection or abnormality in the mouth
- He has been vomiting, has had diarrhea or has been constipated for over 24 hours; call immediately if you notice blood
- He has refused food for over 24 hours
- His eating habits, water intake or toilet habits have noticeably changed; if you have noticed weight gain or weight loss
- He shows symptoms of bloat, which requires *immediate* attention
- He is salivating excessively
- He has a lump in his throat
- He has a lump or bumps anywhere on the body
- He is very lethargic
- He appears to be in pain or otherwise has trouble chewing or swallowing
- His skin loses elasticity

Of course, there will be other instances in which a visit to the vet is necessary; these are just some of the signs that could be indicative of serious problems that need to be caught as early as possible.

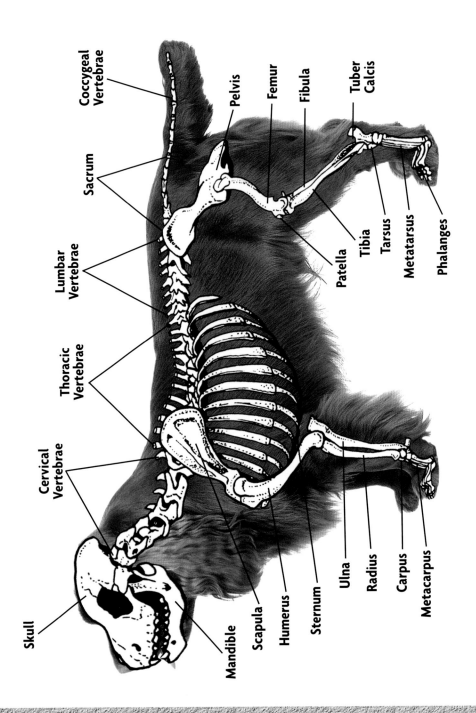

Coccygeal Vertebrae

Pelvis

Femur

Fibula

Tuber Calcis

Sacrum

Tibia

Tarsus

Metatarsus

Phalanges

Patella

Lumbar Vertebrae

Thoracic Vertebrae

Cervical Vertebrae

Skull

Mandible

Scapula

Humerus

Sternum

Ulna

Radius

Carpus

Metacarpus

SKELETAL STRUCTURE OF THE SUSSEX SPANIEL

not sound very important, but most dogs have active periodontal disease by four years of age if they don't have their teeth cleaned regularly at home, not just at their veterinary exams. Dental problems lead to more than just bad "doggy breath." Gum disease can have very serious medical consequences. If you start brushing your dog's teeth and using antiseptic rinses from a young age, your dog will be accustomed to it and will not resist. The results will be healthy dentition, which your pet will need to enjoy a long, healthy life.

Most dogs are considered adults at a year of age, although the Sussex Spaniel continues filling out until about three years of age. Even individual dogs within each breed have different healthcare requirements, so work with your veterinarian to determine

what will be needed and what your role should be. This doctor-client relationship is important, because as vaccination guidelines change, there may not be an annual "vaccine visit" scheduled. You must make sure that you see your veterinarian at least annually, even if no vaccines are due, because this is the best opportunity to coordinate healthcare activities and to make sure that no medical issues creep by unaddressed.

At around age seven or as determined by your vet, your Sussex will be considered a "senior" and likely will require some special care. In general, if you've been taking great care of your canine companion throughout his formative and adult years, the transition to senior status should be a smooth one. Age is not a disease, and as long as everything is functioning as it should, there is no reason why most of late adulthood should not be rewarding for both you and your pet. This is especially true if you have tended to the details, such as regular veterinary visits, proper dental care, excellent nutrition and management of bone and joint issues.

At this stage in your Sussex's life, your veterinarian should want to schedule visits twice yearly, instead of once, to run some laboratory screenings, electrocardiograms and the like, and to change

DENTAL WARNING SIGNS

A veterinary dental exam is necessary if you notice one or any combination of the following in your dog:

- Broken, loose or missing teeth
- Loss of appetite (which could be due to mouth pain or illness caused by infection)
- Gum abnormalities, including redness, swelling and bleeding
- Drooling, with or without blood
- Yellowing of the teeth or gumline, indicating tartar
- Bad breath

the diet to something more digestible. Catching problems early is the best way to manage them effectively. Treating the early stages of heart disease is so much easier than trying to intervene when there is more significant damage to the heart muscle. Similarly, managing the beginning of kidney problems is fairly routine if there is no significant kidney damage. Other problems, like cognitive dysfunction (similar to senility and Alzheimer's disease), cancer,

TAKING YOUR DOG'S TEMPERATURE

It is important to know how to take your dog's temperature at times when you think he may be ill. It's not the most enjoyable task, but it can be done without too much difficulty. It's easier with a helper, preferably someone with whom the dog is friendly, so that one of you can hold the dog while the other inserts the thermometer.

Before inserting the thermometer, coat the end with petroleum jelly. Insert the thermometer slowly and gently into the dog's rectum about one inch. Wait for the reading, about two minutes. Be sure to remove the thermometer carefully and clean it thoroughly after each use.

A dog's normal body temperature is between 100.5 and 102.5 degrees F. Immediate veterinary attention is required if the dog's temperature is below 99 or above 104 degrees F.

diabetes and arthritis, are more common in older dogs, but all can be treated to help the dog live as many happy, comfortable years as possible. Just as in people, medical management is more effective (and less expensive) when you catch things early.

SELECTING A VETERINARIAN

There is probably no more important decision that you will make regarding your pet's healthcare than the selection of his doctor. Your pet's veterinarian will be a pediatrician, family-practice physician and gerontologist, depending on the dog's life stage, and will be the individual who makes recommendations regarding issues such as when specialists need to be consulted, when diagnostic testing and/or therapeutic intervention is needed and when you will need to seek outside emergency and critical-care services. Your vet will act as your advocate and liaison throughout these processes.

Everyone has his own idea about what to look for in a vet, an individual who will play a big role in his dog's (and, of course, his own) life for many years to come. For some, it is the compassionate caregiver with whom they hope to develop a professional relationship to span the lives of their dogs and even their future pets. For others, they are seeking a clinician with keen diagnostic and therapeutic insight who can deliver state-of-the-art healthcare. Still others need a veterinary facility that is open evenings and weekends, is in close proximity or provides mobile veterinary services to accommodate their schedules; these people may not much mind that their dogs might see different veterinarians on each visit. Just as we have different reasons for selecting our own healthcare professionals (e.g., covered by insurance plan, expert in field, convenient location, etc.), we should not expect that there is a one-size-fits-all recommendation for selecting a veterinarian and veterinary practice. The best advice is to be honest in your assessment of what you expect from a veterinary practice and to conscientiously research the options in your area. You will quickly appreciate that not all veterinary practices are the same, and you will be happiest with one that truly meets your needs.

There is another point to be considered in the selection of veterinary services. Not that long ago, a single veterinarian would attempt to manage all medical and surgical issues as they arose. That was often problematic, because veterinarians are trained in many species and many diseases, and it was just impossible for general veterinary practitioners to be experts in every species, every breed, every field and every ailment. However, just as in the human healthcare fields, special-

---

PROBLEM: AND THAT STARTS WITH "P"

Urinary tract problems more commonly affect female dogs, especially those who have been spayed. The first sign that a urinary tract problem exists usually is a strong odor from the urine or an unusual color. Blood in the urine, known as hematuria, is another sign of an infection, related to cystitis, a bladder infection, bladder cancer or a blood-clotting disorder. Urinary tract problems can also be signaled by the dog's straining while urinating, experiencing pain during urination and genital discharge as well as excessive water intake and urination.

Excessive drinking, in and of itself, does not indicate a urinary tract problem. A dog who is drinking more than normal may have a kidney or liver problem, a hormonal disorder or diabetes mellitus. Behaviorists report a disorder known as psychogenic polydipsia, which manifests itself in excessive drinking and urination. If you notice your dog drinking much more than normal, take him to the vet.

---

ization has allowed general practitioners to concentrate on primary healthcare delivery, especially wellness and the prevention of infectious diseases, and to utilize a network of specialists to assist in the management of conditions that require specific expertise and experience. Thus there are now many types of veterinary specialists, including dermatologists, cardiologists, ophthalmologists, surgeons, internists, oncologists, neurologists, behaviorists, criticalists and others to help primary-care veterinarians deal with complicated medical challenges. In most cases, specialists see cases referred by primary-care veterinarians, make diagnoses and set up management plans. From there, the animals' ongoing care is returned to their primary-care veterinarians. This important team approach to your pet's medical-care needs has provided opportunities for advanced care and an unparalleled level of quality to be delivered.

With all of the opportunities for your Sussex to receive high-quality veterinary medical care, there is another topic that needs to be addressed at the same time—cost. It's been said that you can have excellent healthcare or inexpensive healthcare, but never both; this is as true in veterinary medicine as it is in human medicine. While veterinary costs are a fraction of what the same services cost in the human healthcare arena, it is still difficult to deal with unanticipated medical costs, especially since they can easily creep into hundreds or even thousands of

FOOD ALLERGY

Severe itching, leading to bald patches and open sores on the feet, face, ears, armpits and groin, could be caused by a food allergy. Studies indicate that up to 10% of dogs suffer from food allergies, which can develop slowly over time without a change in diet. Dogs who suffer from chronic ear problems may actually have a food allergy. Unfortunately, there are no tests available to determine whether your dog definitely suffers from a food allergy. The dog will be miserable and you will be frustrated and stressed.

Take the problem into your own hands and kitchen. Select a type of meat that your dog is not getting from his existing diet, perhaps white fish, lamb or venison, and prepare a home-cooked food. The food should consist of two parts carbohydrate (rice, pasta or potatoes) and one part protein (the chosen meat). It's better not to start with soy as the protein source unless all of the meats cause a reaction.

Monitor your dog's intake carefully. He must eat only your prepared meal without any treats or side-trips to the garbage can. All family members (and visiting friends) must be informed of the plan. After four or five weeks on the new diet, you will reintroduce a portion of his original diet to determine whether this food is the cause of the skin irritation (or other reactions). Once the dog reacts to the change in diet, resume the new diet. Make dietary modifications every two weeks and keep careful records of any reactions the dog has to the diet.

dollars if specialists or emergency services become involved. However, there are ways of managing these risks. The easiest is to buy pet health insurance and realize that its foremost purpose is not to cover routine healthcare visits but rather to serve as an umbrella for those rainy days when your pet needs medical care and you don't want to worry about whether or not you can afford that care.

Pet insurance policies are very cost-effective (and very inexpensive by human health-insurance standards), but make sure that you buy the policy long before you intend to use it (preferably starting in puppyhood, because coverage will exclude pre-existing conditions) and that you are actually buying an indemnity insurance plan from an insurance company that is regulated by your state or province. Many insurance policy look-alikes are actually discount clubs that are redeemable only at specific locations and for specific services. An indemnity plan covers your pet at almost all veterinary, specialty and emergency practices and is an excellent way to manage your pet's ongoing healthcare needs.

VACCINATIONS AND INFECTIOUS DISEASES

There has never been an easier time to prevent a variety of infectious diseases in your dog, but the advances we've made in veterinary

Time spent outdoors is enjoyable for both dog and owner, but be aware of the allergens, insects and other irritants that your dog can encounter. Always check his skin and coat carefully and report any abnormalities to your vet.

medicine come with a price—choice. Now while it may seem that this choice is a good thing (and it is), it has never been more difficult for the pet owner (or the veterinarian) to make an informed decision about the best way to protect pets through vaccination.

Years ago, it was just accepted that puppies got a starter series of vaccinations and then annual "boosters" throughout their lives to keep them protected. As more and more vaccines became available, consumers wanted the convenience of having all of that protection in a single injection. The result was "multivalent" vaccines that crammed a lot of protection into a single syringe. The manufacturers' recommendations were to give the vaccines annually, and this was a simple enough protocol to follow. However, as veterinary medicine has become more sophisticated and we have started looking more at healthcare quandaries rather than convenience, it became necessary to reevaluate the situation and deal with some tough questions. It is important to realize that whether or not to use a particular vaccine depends on the risk of contracting the disease against which it protects, the severity of the disease if it is contracted, the duration of immunity provided by the vaccine, the safety of the product and the needs of the individual animal. In a very general sense, rabies, distemper, hepatitis and parvovirus are considered core vaccine needs, while parainfluenza, *Bordetella bronchiseptica*, leptospirosis, coronavirus and borreliosis (Lyme disease) are considered non-core needs and best reserved for animals that demonstrate reasonable risk of contracting the diseases.

NEUTERING/SPAYING

Sterilization procedures (neutering for males/spaying for females) are meant to accomplish several purposes. While the underlying premise is to address the risk of pet overpopulation, there are also some medical and behavioral benefits to the surgeries. For females, spaying prior to the first estrus (heat cycle) leads to a marked reduction in the risk of mammary cancer and other serious female health problems. There also will be no manifestations of "heat" to attract male dogs and no bleeding in the house. For males, there is prevention of testicular cancer and a reduction in the risk of prostate problems. In both sexes there may be some limited reduc-

SPAY'S THE WAY

Although spaying a female dog qualifies as major surgery—an ovariohysterectomy, in fact—this procedure is regarded as routine when performed by a qualified veterinarian on a healthy dog. The advantages to spaying a bitch are many and great. Spayed dogs do not develop uterine cancer or any life-threatening diseases of the genitals. Likewise, spayed dogs are at a significantly reduced risk of breast cancer. Bitches (and owners) are relieved of the demands of heat cycles. A spayed bitch will not leave bloody stains on your furniture during estrus, and you will not have to contend with single-minded macho males trying to climb your fence in order to seduce her. The spayed bitch's coat will not show the ill effects of her estrogen level's climbing such as a dull, lackluster outer coat or patches of hairlessness.

tion in aggressive behaviors toward other dogs, and some diminishing of urine marking, roaming and mounting.

While neutering and spaying do indeed prevent animals from contributing to pet overpopulation, even no-cost and low-cost neutering options have not eliminated the problem. Perhaps one of the main reasons for this is that individuals that intentionally breed their dogs and those that allow their animals to run at large are the main causes of unwanted offspring. Also, animals in shelters are often there because they were abandoned or relinquished, not because they came from unplanned matings. Neutering/ spaying is important, but it should be considered in the context of the real causes of animals' ending up in shelters and eventually being euthanized.

One of the important considerations regarding neutering is that it is a surgical procedure. This sometimes gets lost in discussions of low-cost procedures and commoditization of the process. In females, spaying is specifically referred to as an ovariohysterectomy. In this procedure, a midline incision is made in the abdomen and the entire uterus and both ovaries are surgically removed. While this is a major invasive surgical procedure, it usually has few complications, because it is typically performed

on healthy young animals. However, it is major surgery, as any woman who has had a hysterectomy will attest.

In males, neutering has traditionally referred to castration, which involves the surgical removal of both testicles. While still a significant piece of surgery, there is not the abdominal exposure that is required in the female surgery. In addition, there is now a chemical sterilization option, in which a solution is injected into each testicle, leading to atrophy of the sperm-producing cells. This can typically be done under sedation rather than full anesthesia. This is a relatively new approach, and there are no long-term clinical studies yet available.

Neutering/spaying is typically done around six months of age at most veterinary hospitals, although techniques have been pioneered to perform the procedures in animals as young as eight weeks of age. In general, the surgeries on the very young animals are done for the specific reason of sterilizing them before they go to their new homes. This is done in some shelter hospitals for assurance that the animals will definitely not produce any pups. Otherwise, these organizations need to rely on owners to comply with their wishes to have the animals "altered" at a later date, something that does not always happen.

A scanning electron micrograph of a dog flea, Ctenocephalides canis, on dog hair.

EXTERNAL PARASITES

FLEAS

Fleas have been around for millions of years and, while we have better tools now for controlling them than at any time in the past, there still is little chance that they will end up on an endangered species list. Actually, they are very well adapted to living on our pets, and they continue to adapt as we make advances.

The female flea can consume 15 times her weight in blood during active reproduction and can lay as many as 40 eggs a day. These eggs are very resistant to the effects of insecticides. They hatch into larvae, which then mature and spin cocoons. The immature fleas reside in this pupal stage until the time is right for feeding. This pupal stage is also very resistant to the effects of insecticides, and pupae can last in the environment without feeding for many months. Newly emergent fleas are attracted to animals by the warmth of the animals' bodies, movement and exhaled carbon dioxide. However, when they first emerge from their cocoons, they orient towards light; thus when an animal passes between a flea and the light source, casting a shadow, the flea pounces and starts to feed. If the animal turns out to be a dog or cat, the reproductive cycle continues. If the flea lands on another type of animal, including a person, the flea will bite but will then look for a more appropriate host. An emerging adult flea can survive without feeding for up to 12 months but, once it tastes blood, it can survive off its host for only 3 to 4 days.

It was once thought that fleas spend most of their lives in the environment, but we now know that fleas won't willingly jump off a dog unless leaping to another dog or when physically removed by brushing, bathing or other manipulation. Flea eggs, on the other hand, are shiny and smooth, and they roll off the animal and into the environment. The eggs, larvae and pupae then exist in the environment, but once the adult finds a susceptible animal, it's home sweet home until the flea is forced to seek refuge elsewhere.

Since adult fleas live on the animal and immature forms survive in the environment, a successful treatment plan must address all stages of the flea life cycle. There are now several safe and effective flea-control products that can be applied on a monthly

FLEA PREVENTION FOR YOUR DOG

- Discuss with your veterinarian the safest product to protect your dog, likely in the form of a monthly tablet or a liquid preparation placed on the back of the dog's neck.
- For dogs suffering from flea-bite dermatitis, a shampoo or topical insecticide treatment is required.
- Your lawn and property should be sprayed with an insecticide designed to kill fleas and ticks that lurk outdoors.
- Using a flea comb, check the dog's coat regularly for any signs of parasites.
- Practice good housekeeping. Vacuum floors, carpets and furniture regularly, especially in the areas that the dog frequents, and wash the dog's bedding weekly.
- Follow up house-cleaning with carpet shampoos and sprays to rid the house of fleas at all stages of development. Insect growth regulators are the safest option.

basis. These include fipronil, imidacloprid, selamectin and permethrin (found in several formulations). Most of these products have significant flea-killing rates within 24 hours. However, none of them will control the immature forms in the environment. To accomplish this, there are a variety of insect growth regulators that can be sprayed into

THE FLEA'S LIFE CYCLE

What came first, the flea or the egg? This age-old mystery is more difficult to comprehend than the actual cycle of the flea. Fleas usually live only about four months. A female can lay 2,000 eggs in her lifetime.

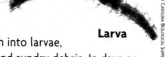

Egg

After ten days of rolling around your carpet or under your furniture, the eggs hatch into larvae, which feed on various and sundry debris. In days or months, depending on the climate, the larvae spin cocoons and develop into the pupal or nymph stage, which quickly develop into fleas.

Larva

Pupa

These immature fleas must locate a host within 10 to 14 days or they will die. Only about 1% of the flea population exist as adult fleas, while the other 99% exist as eggs, larvae or pupae.

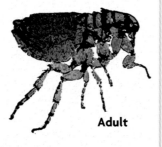

Adult

PHOTO BY CAROLINA BIOLOGICAL SUPPLY CO.

KILL FLEAS THE NATURAL WAY

If you choose not to go the route of conventional medication, there are some natural ways to ward off fleas:

- Dust your dog with a natural flea powder, composed of such herbal goodies as rosemary, wormwood, pennyroyal, citronella, rue, tobacco powder and eucalyptus.
- Apply diatomaceous earth, the fossilized remains of single-cell algae, to your carpets, furniture and pet's bedding. Even though it's not good for dogs, it's even worse for fleas, which will dry up swiftly and die.
- Brush your dog frequently, give him adequate exercise and let him fast occasionally. All of these activities strengthen the dog's immune system and make him more resistant to disease and parasites.
- Bathe your dog with a capful of pennyroyal or eucalyptus oil.
- Feed a natural diet, free of additives and preservatives. Add a little fresh garlic and brewer's yeast to the dog's morning portion, as these items have flea-repelling properties.

the environment (e.g., pyriproxyfen, methoprene, fenoxycarb) as well as insect development inhibitors such as lufenuron that can be administered. These compounds have no effect on adult fleas, but they stop immature forms from developing into

adults. In years gone by, we relied heavily on toxic insecticides (such as organophosphates, organochlorines and carbamates) to manage the flea problem, but today's options are not only much safer to use on our pets but also safer for the environment.

TICKS

Ticks are members of the spider class (arachnids) and are blood-sucking parasites capable of transmitting a variety of diseases, including Lyme disease, ehrlichiosis, babesiosis and Rocky Mountain spotted fever. It's easy to see ticks on your own skin, but it is more of a challenge when your furry companion is affected. Whenever you happen to be planning a stroll in a tick-infested area (especially forests, grassy or wooded areas or parks) be prepared to do a thorough inspection of your dog afterward to search for ticks. Ticks can be tricky, so make sure you spend time looking in the ears, between the toes and everywhere else where a tick might hide. Ticks need to be attached for 24–72 hours before they transmit most of the diseases that they carry, so you do have a window of opportunity for some preventive intervention.

A TICKING BOMB

There is nothing good about a tick's harpooning his nose into your dog's skin. Among the diseases caused by ticks are Rocky Mountain spotted fever, canine ehrlichiosis, canine babesiosis, canine hepatozoonosis and Lyme disease. If a dog is allergic to the saliva of a female wood tick, he can develop tick paralysis.

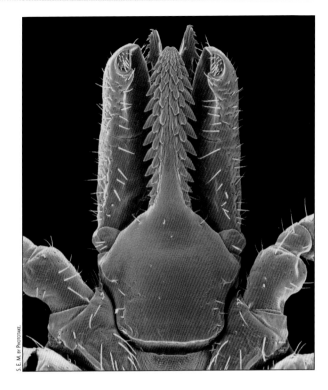

S. E. M. BY PHOTOTAKE.

Female ticks live to eat and breed. They can lay between 4,000 and 5,000 eggs and they die soon after. Males, on the other hand, live only to mate with the females and continue the process as long as they are able. Most ticks live on multiple hosts before parasitizing dogs. The immature forms typically reside on grass and shrubs, waiting for susceptible animals to walk by. The larvae and nymph stages typically feed on wildlife.

If only a few ticks are present on a dog, they can be plucked out, but it is important to remove the entire head and mouthparts,

A scanning electron micrograph of the head of a female deer tick, *Ixodes dammini*, a parasitic tick that carries Lyme disease.

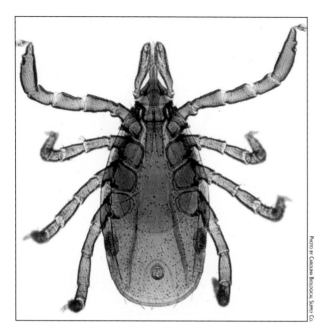

PHOTO BY CAROLINA BIOLOGICAL SUPPLY CO.

**Deer tick,
Ixodes dammini.**

which may be deeply embedded in the skin. This is best accomplished with forceps designed especially for this purpose; fingers can be used but should be protected with rubber gloves, plastic wrap or at least a paper towel. The tick should be grasped as closely as possible to the animal's skin and should be pulled upward with steady, even pressure. Do not squeeze, crush or puncture the body of the tick or you risk exposure to any disease carried by that tick. Once the ticks have been removed, the sites of attachment should be disinfected. Your hands should then be washed with soap and water to further minimize risk of contagion. The tick should be disposed of in a container of alcohol or household bleach.

Some of the newer flea products, specifically those with fipronil, selamectin and permethrin, have effect against some, but not all, species of tick. Flea collars containing appropriate pesticides (e.g., propoxur, chlorfenvinphos) can aid in tick control. In most areas, such collars should be placed on animals in March, at the beginning of the tick season, and changed regularly. Leaving the collar on when the pesticide level is waning invites the development of resistance. Amitraz collars are also good for tick control, and the active ingredient does not interfere with other flea-control products. The ingredient helps prevent the attachment of ticks to the skin and will cause those ticks already on the skin to detach themselves.

TICK CONTROL

Removal of underbrush and leaf litter and the thinning of trees in areas where tick control is desired are recommended. These actions remove the cover and food sources for small animals that serve as hosts for ticks. With continued mowing of grasses in these areas, the probability of ticks' surviving is further reduced. A variety of insecticide ingredients (e.g., resmethrin, carbaryl, permethrin, chlorpyrifos, dioxathion and allethrin) are registered for tick control around the home.

MITES

Mites are tiny arachnid parasites that parasitize the skin of dogs. Skin diseases caused by mites are referred to as "mange," and there are many different forms seen in dogs. These forms are very different from one another, each one warranting an individual description.

Sarcoptic mange, or scabies, is one of the itchiest conditions that affects dogs. The microscopic *Sarcoptes* mites burrow into the superficial layers of the skin and can drive dogs crazy with itchiness. They are also communicable to people, although they can't complete their reproductive cycle on people. In addition to being tiny, the mites also are often difficult to find when trying to make a diagnosis. Skin scrapings from multiple areas are examined microscopically but, even then, sometimes the mites cannot be found.

Fortunately, scabies is relatively easy to treat, and there are a variety of products that will successfully kill the mites. Since the mites can't live in the environment for very long without feeding, a complete cure is usually possible within four to eight weeks.

Cheyletiellosis is caused by a relatively large mite, which sometimes can be seen even without a microscope. Often referred to as "walking dandruff," this also causes itching, but not usually as profound as with scabies. While *Cheyletiella* mites can survive somewhat longer

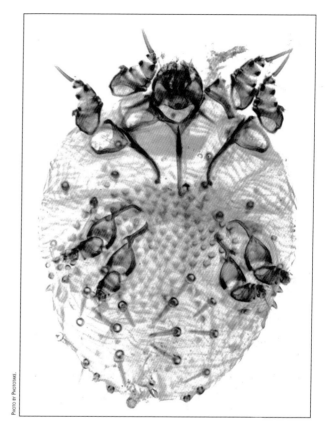

PHOTO BY PHOTOTAKE.

Sarcoptes scabiei, commonly known as the "itch mite."

in the environment than scabies mites, they too are relatively easy to treat, being responsive to not only the medications used to treat scabies but also often to flea-control products.

Otodectes cynotis is the canine ear mite and is one of the more common causes of mange, especially in young dogs in shelters or pet stores. That's because the mites are typically present in large numbers and are quickly spread to nearby animals. The mites rarely do much harm but

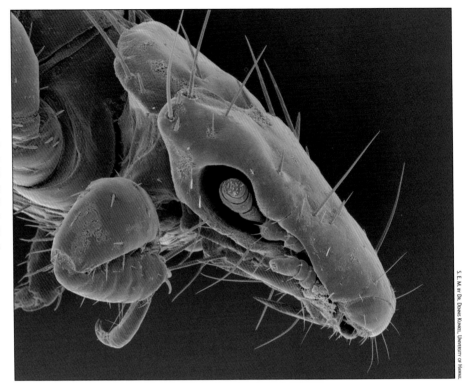

Micrograph of a dog louse, *Heterodoxus spiniger*. Female lice attach their eggs to the hairs of the dog. As the eggs hatch, the larval lice bite and feed on the blood. Lice can also feed on dead skin and hair. This feeding activity can cause hair loss and skin problems.

S. E. M. by Dr. Dennis Kunkel, University of Hawaii

can be difficult to eradicate if the treatment regimen is not comprehensive. While many try to treat the condition with ear drops only, this is the most common cause of treatment failure. Ear drops cause the mites to simply move out of the ears and as far away as possible (usually to the base of the tail) until the insecticide levels in the ears drop to an acceptable level—then it's back to business as usual! The successful treatment of ear mites requires treating all animals in the household with a systemic insecticide, such as selamectin, or a combination of miticidal ear drops combined with whole-body flea-control preparations.

Demodicosis, sometimes referred to as red mange, can be one of the most difficult forms of mange to treat. Part of the problem has to do with the fact that the mites live in the hair follicles and they are relatively well shielded from topical and systemic products. The main issue, however, is that demodectic mange typically results only when there is some underlying process interfering with the dog's immune system.

Since *Demodex* mites are normal residents of the skin of

mammals, including humans, there is usually a mite population explosion only when the immune system fails to keep the number of mites in check. In young animals, the immune deficit may be transient or may reflect an actual inherited immune problem. In older animals, demodicosis is usually seen only when there is another disease hampering the immune system, such as diabetes, cancer, thyroid problems or the use of immune-suppressing drugs. Accordingly, treatment involves not only trying to kill the mange mites but also discerning what is interfering with immune function and correcting it if possible.

Chiggers represent several different species of mite that don't parasitize dogs specifically, but do latch on to passersby and can cause irritation. The problem is most prevalent in wooded areas in the late summer and fall. Treatment is not difficult, as the mites do not complete their life cycle on dogs and are susceptible to a variety of miticidal products.

MOSQUITOES

Mosquitoes have long been known to transmit a variety of diseases to people, as well as just being biting pests during warm weather. They also pose a real risk to pets. Not only do they carry deadly heartworms but recently there also has been much concern over their involvement with West Nile virus. While we can avoid heartworm with the use of preventive medications, there are no such preventives for West Nile virus. The only method of prevention in endemic areas is active mosquito control. Fortunately, most dogs that have been exposed to the virus only developed flu-like symptoms and, to date, there have not been the large number of reported deaths in canines as seen in some other species.

Illustration of *Demodex folliculoram.*

ILLUSTRATION BY PHOTODISC.

MOSQUITO REPELLENT

Low concentrations of DEET (less than 10%), found in many human mosquito repellents, have been safely used on dogs but, in these concentrations, probably give only about two hours of protection. DEET may be safe in these small concentrations, but since it is not licensed for use on dogs, there is no research proving its safety for dogs. Products containing permethrin give the longest-lasting protection, perhaps two to four weeks. As DEET is not licensed for use on dogs, and both DEET and permethrin can be quite toxic to cats, appropriate care should be exercised. Other products, such as those containing oil of citronella, also have some mosquito-repellent activity, but typically have a relatively short duration of action.

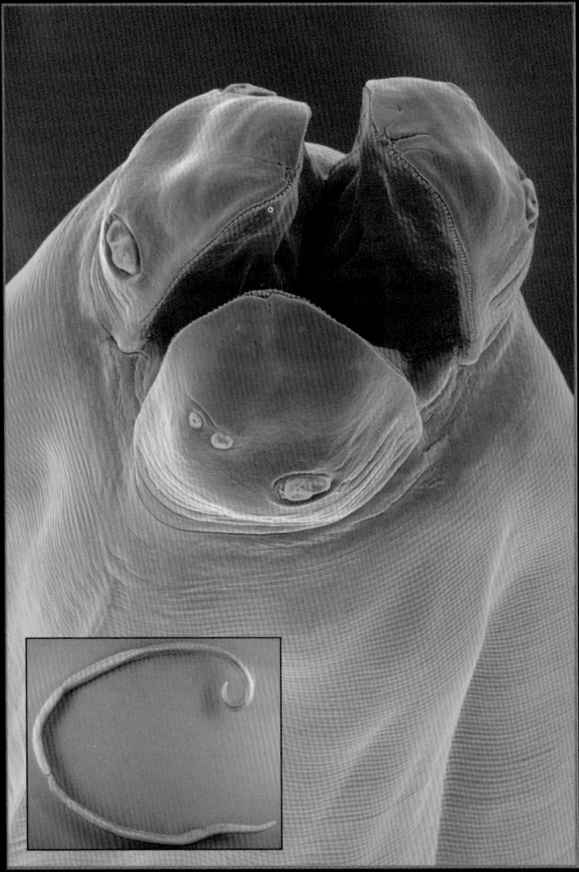

S. E. M. by Dr. Dennis Kunkel, University of Hawaii; Inset by Tam C. Nguyen.

ASCARID DANGERS

The most commonly encountered worms in dogs are roundworms known as ascarids. *Toxascaris leonine* and *Toxocara canis* are the two species that infect dogs. Subsisting in the dog's stomach and intestines, adult roundworms can grow to 7 inches in length and adult females can lay in excess of 200,000 eggs in a single day.

In humans, visceral larval migrans affects people who have ingested eggs of *Toxocara canis*, which frequently contaminates children's sandboxes, beaches and park grounds. The roundworms reside in the human's stomach and intestines, as they would in a dog's, but do not mature. Instead, they find their way to the liver, lungs and skin, or even to the heart or kidneys in severe cases. Deworming puppies is critical in preventing the infection in humans, and young children should never handle nursing pups who have not been dewormed.

The ascarid roundworm *Toxocara canis*, showing the mouth with three lips. INSET: Photomicrograph of the roundworm *Ascaris lumbricoides*.

INTERNAL PARASITES: WORMS

Ascarids

Ascarids are intestinal roundworms that rarely cause severe disease in dogs. Nonetheless, they are of major public health significance because they can be transferred to people. Sadly, it is children who are most commonly affected by the parasite, probably from inadvertently ingesting ascarid-contaminated soil. In fact, many yards and children's sandboxes contain appreciable numbers of ascarid eggs. So, while ascarids don't bite dogs or latch onto their intestines to suck blood, they do cause some nasty medical conditions in children and are best eradicated from our furry friends. Because pups can start passing ascarid eggs by three weeks of age, most parasite-control programs begin at two weeks of age and are repeated every two weeks until pups are eight weeks old. It is important to

HOOKED ON ANCYLOSTOMA

Adult dogs can become infected by the bloodsucking nematodes we commonly call hookworms via ingesting larvae from the ground or via the larvae penetrating the dog's skin. It is not uncommon for infected dogs to show no symptoms of hookworm infestation. Sometimes symptoms occur within ten days of exposure. These symptoms can include bloody diarrhea, anemia, loss of weight and general weakness. Dogs pass the hookworm eggs in their stools, which serves as the vet's method of identifying the infestation. The hookworm larvae can encyst themselves in the dog's tissues and be released when the dog is experiencing stress.

Caused by an *Ancylostoma* species whose common host is the dog, cutaneous larval migrans affects humans, causing itching and lumps and streaks beneath the surface of the skin.

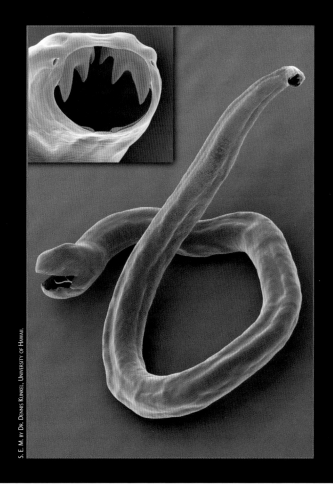

S. E. M. BY DR. DENNIS KUNKEL, UNIVERSITY OF HAWAII.

realize that bitches can pass ascarids to their pups even if they test negative prior to whelping. Accordingly, bitches are best treated at the same time as the pups.

HOOKWORMS

Unlike ascarids, hookworms do latch onto a dog's intestinal tract and can cause significant loss of blood and protein. Similar to ascarids, hookworms can be transmitted to humans, where they cause a condition known as cutaneous larval migrans. Dogs can become infected either by consuming the infective larvae or by the larvae's penetrating the skin directly. People most often get infected when they are lying on the ground (such as on a beach) and the larvae penetrate the skin. Yes, the larvae can penetrate through a beach blanket. Hookworms are typically susceptible to the same medications used to treat ascarids.

The hookworm *Ancylostoma caninum* infests the intestines of dogs. INSET: Note the row of hooks at the posterior end, used to anchor the worm to the intestinal wall.

WHIPWORMS

Whipworms latch onto the lower aspects of the dog's colon and can cause cramping and diarrhea. Eggs do not start to appear in the dog's feces until about three months after the dog was infected. This worm has a peculiar life cycle, which makes it more difficult to control than ascarids or hookworms. The good thing is that whipworms rarely are transferred to people.

Some of the medications used to treat ascarids and hookworms are also effective against whipworms, but, in general, a separate treatment protocol is needed. Since most of the medications are effective against the adults but not the eggs or larvae, treatment is typically repeated in three weeks, and then often in three

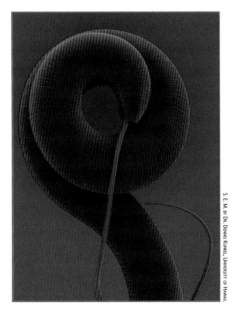

Adult whipworm,
Trichuris sp., an
intestinal
parasite.

S. E. M. BY DR. DENNIS KUNKEL, UNIVERSITY OF HAWAII.

> **WORM-CONTROL GUIDELINES**
> - Practice sanitary habits with your dog and home.
> - Clean up after your dog and don't let him sniff or eat other dogs' droppings.
> - Control insects and fleas in the dog's environment. Fleas, lice, cockroaches, beetles, mice and rats can act as hosts for various worms.
> - Prevent dogs from eating uncooked meat, raw poultry and dead animals.
> - Keep dogs and children from playing in sand and soil.
> - Kennel dogs on cement or gravel; avoid dirt runs.
> - Administer heartworm preventives regularly.
> - Have your vet examine your dog's stools at your annual visits.
> - Select a boarding kennel carefully so as to avoid contamination from other dogs or an unsanitary environment.
> - Prevent dogs from roaming. Obey local leash laws.

months as well. Unfortunately, since dogs don't develop resistance to whipworms, it is difficult to prevent them from getting reinfected if they visit soil contaminated with whipworm eggs.

TAPEWORMS

There are many different species of tapeworm that affect dogs, but *Dipylidium caninum* is probably the most common and is spread by fleas. Flea larvae feed on organic debris and tapeworm eggs in the environment and, when a dog chews at himself and manages to ingest fleas, he might get a dose of tapeworm at the same time. The tapeworm then develops further in the intestine of the dog.

The tapeworm itself, which is a parasitic flatworm that latches onto the intestinal wall, is composed of numerous segments. When the segments break off into the intestine (as proglottids), they may accumulate around the rectum, like grains of rice. While this tapeworm is disgusting in its behavior, it is not directly communicable to humans (although humans can also get infected by swallowing fleas).

A much more dangerous tapeworm is *Echinococcus multilocularis*, which is typically found in foxes, coyotes and wolves. The eggs are passed in the feces and infect rodents, and, when dogs eat the rodents, the dogs can be infected by thousands of adult tapeworms. While the parasites don't cause many problems in dogs, this is considered the most lethal worm infection that people can get. Take appropriate precautions if you live in an area in which these tapeworms are found. Do not use mulch that may contain feces of dogs, cats or wildlife, and discourage your pets from hunting wildlife. Treat these tapeworm infections aggressively in pets, because if humans get infected, approximately half die.

HEARTWORMS

Heartworm disease is caused by the parasite *Dirofilaria immitis* and is seen in dogs around the world. A member of the roundworm group, it is spread between dogs by the bite of an infected mosquito. The mosquito injects infective larvae into the dog's skin with its bite, and these larvae develop under the skin for a period of time before making their way to the heart. There they develop into adults, which grow and create blockages of the heart, lungs and major blood vessels there. They also start producing offspring (microfilariae),

A dog tapeworm proglottid (body segment).

The dog tapeworm *Taenia pisiformis.*

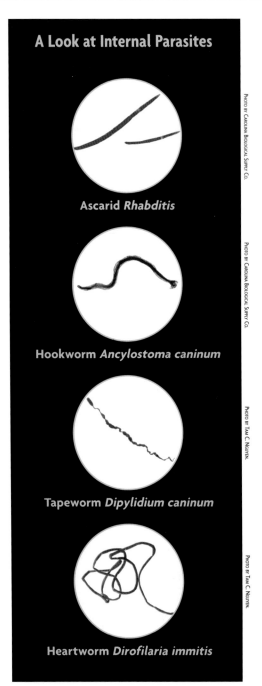

A Look at Internal Parasites

Ascarid *Rhabditis*

Hookworm *Ancylostoma caninum*

Tapeworm *Dipylidium caninum*

Heartworm *Dirofilaria immitis*

and these microfilariae circulate in the bloodstream, waiting to hitch a ride when the next mosquito bites. Once in the mosquito, the microfilariae develop into infective larvae and the entire process is repeated.

When dogs get infected with heartworm, over time they tend to develop symptoms associated with heart disease, such as coughing, exercise intolerance and potentially many other manifestations. Diagnosis is confirmed by either seeing the microfilariae themselves in blood samples or using immunologic tests (antigen testing) to identify the presence of adult heartworms. Since antigen tests measure the presence of adult heartworms and microfilarial tests measure offspring produced by adults, neither are positive until six to seven months after the initial infection. However, the beginning of damage can occur by fifth-stage larvae as early as three months after infection. Thus it is possible for dogs to be harboring problem-causing larvae for up to three months before either type of test would identify an infection.

The good news is that there are great protocols available for preventing heartworm in dogs. Testing is critical in the process, and it is important to understand the benefits as well as the limitations of such testing. All dogs six months of age or older that have not been on continuous heartworm-preventive medication should be

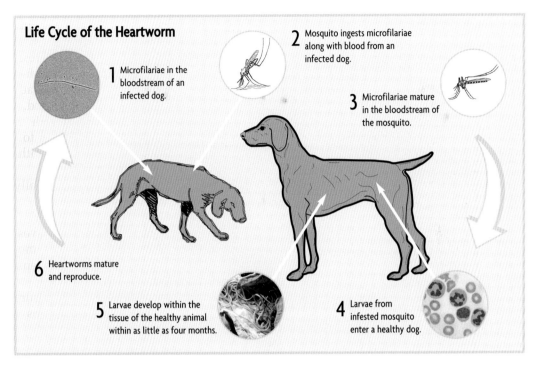

Life Cycle of the Heartworm

1 Microfilariae in the bloodstream of an infected dog.

2 Mosquito ingests microfilariae along with blood from an infected dog.

3 Microfilariae mature in the bloodstream of the mosquito.

4 Larvae from infested mosquito enter a healthy dog.

5 Larvae develop within the tissue of the healthy animal within as little as four months.

6 Heartworms mature and reproduce.

screened with microfilarial or antigen tests. For dogs receiving preventive medication, periodic antigen testing helps assess the effectiveness of the preventives. The American Heartworm Society guidelines suggest that annual retesting may not be necessary when owners have absolutely provided continuous heartworm prevention. Retesting on a two- to three-year interval may be sufficient in these cases. However, your veterinarian will likely have specific guidelines under which heartworm preventives will be prescribed, and many prefer to err on the side of safety and retest annually.

It is indeed fortunate that heartworm is relatively easy to prevent, because treatments can be as life-threatening as the disease itself. Treatment requires a two-step process that kills the adult heartworms first and then the microfilariae. Prevention is obviously preferable; this involves a once-monthly oral or topical treatment. The most common oral preventives include ivermectin (not suitable for some breeds), moxidectin and milbemycin oxime; the once-a-month topical drug selamectin provides heartworm protection in addition to flea, some types of tick and other parasite controls.

THE **ABC**S OF
Emergency Care

Abrasions
Clean wound with running water or 3% hydrogen peroxide. Pat dry with gauze and spray with antibiotic. Do not cover.

Animal Bites
Clean area with soap and saline solution or water. Apply pressure to any bleeding area. Apply antibiotic ointment. Identify biting animal and contact the vet.

Antifreeze Poisoning
Induce vomiting and take dog to the vet.

Bee Sting
Remove stinger and apply soothing lotion or cold compress; give antihistamine in proper dosage.

Bleeding
Apply pressure directly to wound with gauze or towel for five to ten minutes. If wound does not stop bleeding, wrap wound with gauze and adhesive tape.

Bloat/Gastric Torsion
Immediately take the dog to the vet or emergency clinic; phone from car. No time to waste.

Burns
Chemical: Bathe dog with water and pet shampoo. Rinse in saline solution. Apply antibiotic ointment.

Acid: Rinse with water. Apply one part baking soda, two parts water to affected area.

Alkali: Rinse with water. Apply one part vinegar, four parts water to affected area.

Electrical: Apply antibiotic ointment. Seek veterinary assistance immediately.

Choking
If the dog is on the verge of collapsing, wedge a solid object, such as the handle of a screwdriver, between molars on one side of mouth to keep mouth open. Pull tongue out. Use long-nosed pliers or fingers to remove foreign object. Do not push the object down the dog's throat. For small or medium dogs, hold dog upside down by hind legs and shake firmly to dislodge foreign object.

Chlorine Ingestion
With clean water, rinse the mouth and eyes. Give dog water to drink; contact the vet.

Constipation
Feed dog 2 tablespoons bran flakes with each meal. Encourage drinking water. Mix 1/4-teaspoon mineral oil in dog's food. Contact vet if persists longer than 24 hours.

Diarrhea
Withhold food for 12 to 24 hours. Feed dog anti-diarrheal with eyedropper. When feeding resumes, feed one part boiled hamburger, one part plain cooked rice, 1/4 to 3/4-cup four times daily. Contact vet if persists longer than 24 hours.

Dog Bite
Snip away hair around puncture wound; clean with 3% hydrogen peroxide; apply tincture of iodine. Identify biting dog and call the vet. If wound appears deep, take the dog to the vet.

Frostbite
Wrap the dog in a heavy blanket. Warm affected area with a warm bath for ten minutes. Red color to skin will return with circulation; if tissues are pale after 20 minutes, contact the vet.

Use a portable, durable container large enough to contain all items.

Heat Stroke
Submerge the dog (up to his muzzle) in cold water; if no response within ten minutes, contact the vet.

Hot Spots
Mix 2 packets Domeboro® with 2 cups water. Saturate cloth with mixture and apply to hot spots for 15–30 minutes. Apply antibiotic ointment. Repeat every six to eight hours.

Poisonous Plants
Wash affected area with soap and water. Cleanse with alcohol. For foxtail/grass, apply antibiotic ointment. Contact vet if plant was ingested.

Rat Poison Ingestion
Induce vomiting. Keep dog calm, maintain dog's normal body temperature (use blanket or heating pad). Get to the vet for antidote.

Shock
Keep the dog calm and warm; call for veterinary assistance.

Snake Bite
If possible, bandage the area and apply pressure. If the area is not conducive to bandaging, use ice to control bleeding. Get immediate help from the vet.

Tick Removal
Apply flea and tick spray directly on tick. Wait one minute. Using tweezers or wearing plastic gloves, grasp the tick's body firmly and pull out. Apply antibiotic ointment.

Vomiting
Restrict water intake; offer a few ice cubes. Withhold food for next meal. Contact vet if vomiting persists longer than 24 hours.

DOG OWNER'S FIRST-AID KIT
- ❏ **Gauze bandages/swabs**
- ❏ **Adhesive and non-adhesive bandages**
- ❏ **Antibiotic powder**
- ❏ **Antiseptic wash**
- ❏ **Hydrogen peroxide 3%**
- ❏ **Antibiotic ointment**
- ❏ **Lubricating jelly**
- ❏ **Rectal thermometer**
- ❏ **Nylon muzzle**
- ❏ **Scissors and forceps**
- ❏ **Eyedropper**
- ❏ **Syringe**
- ❏ **Anti-bacterial/fungal solution**
- ❏ **Saline solution**
- ❏ **Antihistamine**
- ❏ **Cotton balls**
- ❏ **Nail clippers**
- ❏ **Screwdriver/pen knife**
- ❏ **Flashlight**
- ❏ **Emergency phone numbers**

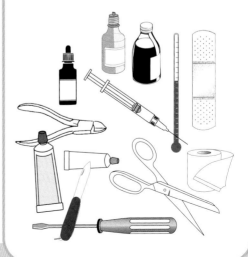

Number-One Killer Disease in Dogs: CANCER

In every age, there is a word associated with a disease or plague that causes humans to shudder. In the 21st century, that word is "cancer." Just as cancer is the leading cause of death in humans, it claims nearly half the lives of dogs that die from a natural disease as well as half the dogs that die over the age of ten years.

Described as a genetic disease, cancer becomes a greater risk as the dog ages. Vets and dog owners have become increasingly aware of the threat of cancer to dogs. Statistics reveal that one dog in every five will develop cancer, the most common of which is skin cancer. Many cancers, including prostate, ovarian and breast cancer, can be avoided by spaying and neutering our dogs by the age of six months.

Early detection of cancer can save or extend a dog's life, so it is absolutely vital for owners to have their dogs examined by a qualified vet or oncologist immediately upon detection of any abnormality. Certain dietary guidelines have also proven to reduce the onset and spread of cancer. Foods based on fish rather than beef, due to the presence of Omega-3 fatty acids, are recommended. Other amino acids such as glutamine have significant benefits for canines, particularly those breeds that show a greater susceptibility to cancer.

Cancer management and treatments promise hope for future generations of canines. Since the disease is genetic, breeders should never breed a dog whose parents, grandparents and any related siblings have developed cancer. It is difficult to know whether to exclude an otherwise healthy dog from a breeding program, as the disease does not manifest itself until the dog's senior years.

RECOGNIZE CANCER WARNING SIGNS

Since early detection can possibly rescue your dog from becoming a cancer statistic, it is essential for owners to recognize the possible signs and seek the assistance of a qualified professional.

- Abnormal bumps or lumps that continue to grow
- Bleeding or discharge from any body cavity
- Persistent stiffness or lameness
- Recurrent sores or sores that do not heal
- Inappetence
- Breathing difficulties
- Weight loss
- Bad breath or odors
- General malaise and fatigue
- Eating and swallowing problems
- Difficulty urinating and defecating

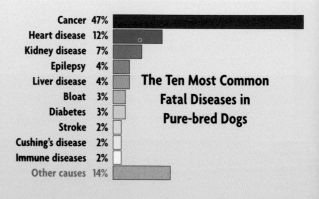

Cancer	47%
Heart disease	12%
Kidney disease	7%
Epilepsy	4%
Liver disease	4%
Bloat	3%
Diabetes	3%
Stroke	2%
Cushing's disease	2%
Immune diseases	2%
Other causes	14%

The Ten Most Common Fatal Diseases in Pure-bred Dogs

CANINE COGNITIVE DYSFUNCTION

"OLD-DOG SYNDROME"

There are many ways for you to evaluate old-dog syndrome. Veterinarians have defined canine cognitive dysfunction as the gradual deterioration of cognitive abilities, indicated by changes in the dog's behavior. When a dog changes his routine response, and maladies have been eliminated as the cause of these behavioral changes, then canine cognitive dysfunction is the usual diagnosis.

More than half the dogs over eight years old suffer from some form of cognitive dysfunction. The older the dog, the more chance he has of suffering from cognitive dysfunction. In humans, doctors often dismiss the cognitive-dysfunction behavioral changes as part of "winding down."

There are four major signs of canine cognitive dysfunction: frequent potty accidents inside the home, sleeping much more or much less than normal, acting confused and failing to respond to social stimuli. There are medications available to help affected dogs.

SYMPTOMS OF CANINE COGNITIVE DYSFUNCTION

FREQUENT POTTY ACCIDENTS
- Urinates in the house.
- Defecates in the house.
- Doesn't signal that he wants to go out.

FAILURE TO RESPOND TO SOCIAL STIMULI
- Comes to people less frequently, whether called or not.
- Doesn't tolerate petting for more than a short time.
- Doesn't come to the door when you return home.

CONFUSION
- Goes outside and just stands there.
- Appears confused with a faraway look in his eyes.
- Hides more often.
- Doesn't recognize friends.
- Doesn't come when called.
- Walks around listlessly and without a destination.

SLEEP PATTERNS
- Awakens more slowly.
- Sleeps more than normal during the day.
- Sleeps less during the night.

SUSSEX SPANIEL

When we bring home a puppy, full of the energy and exuberance that accompanies youth, we hope for a long, happy and fulfilling relationship with the new family member. Even when we adopt an older dog, we look forward to the years of companionship ahead with a new canine friend. However, aging is inevitable for all creatures, and there will come a time when your Sussex reaches his senior years and will need special considerations and attention to his care.

WHEN IS MY DOG A "SENIOR"?
You can make the generalization that Sussex Spaniels have a lifespan of 12 years on the average, with the typical range being between 11 and 15 years. It is probably safe to say that by age 11 years, most Sussex Spaniels are retired or semi-retired from strenuous physical activities, though most appreciate being included in shorter and less strenuous sessions of regular activities such as hunting. Keeping a Sussex Spaniel active as befits his age is recommended for both mental and physical well-being.

The Sussex is considered physically mature at about three years of age. In terms of veterinary care, many veterinarians and behaviorists use the seven-year mark as the time to consider a dog a "senior" and begin a preventive healthcare program designed for older dogs. Obviously, the old "seven dog years to one human year" theory is not exact. In puppyhood, a dog's year is actually comparable to more than seven human years, considering the puppy's rapid growth during his first year. Then, in adulthood, the ratio decreases. Regardless, the more viable rule of thumb is that the larger the dog, the shorter his expected lifespan. Of course, this can vary among individual dogs, with many living longer than expected, which we hope is the case!

WHAT ARE THE SIGNS OF AGING?
By the time your dog has reached his senior years, you will know him very well, so the physical and behavioral changes that accompany aging should be noticeable to you. Humans and

dogs share the most obvious physical sign of aging: gray hair! Graying often occurs first on the muzzle and face, around the eyes. Other telltale signs are the dog's overall decrease in activity. Your older dog might be more content to nap and rest, and he may not show the same old enthusiasm when it's time to play in the yard or go for a walk. Other physical signs include significant weight loss or gain; more labored movement; skin and coat problems, possibly hair loss; sight and/or hearing problems; changes in toileting habits, perhaps seeming "unhousebroken" at times; and tooth decay, bad breath or other mouth problems.

There are behavioral changes that go along with aging, too. There are numerous causes for behavioral changes. Sometimes a dog's apparent confusion results from a physical change like diminished sight or hearing. If his confusion causes him to be afraid, he may act aggressively or defensively. He may sleep more frequently because his daily walks, though shorter now, tire him out. He may begin to experience separation anxiety or, conversely, become less interested in petting and attention.

There also are clinical conditions that cause behavioral changes in older dogs. One such condition is known as canine cognitive dysfunction (familiarly known as "old-dog" syndrome). It can be frustrating for an owner whose dog is affected with cognitive dysfunction, as it can result in behavioral changes of all types, most seemingly unexplainable. Common changes include the dog's forgetting aspects of the daily routine, such as times to eat, go out for walks, relieve himself and the like. Along the same lines, you may take your dog out at the regular time for a potty trip and he may have no idea why he is there. Sometimes a placid dog will begin to show aggressive or possessive tendencies or, conversely, a hyperactive dog will start to "mellow out."

Disease also can be the cause of behavioral changes in senior

A senior Sussex, still alert, in great condition and "sitting pretty."

dogs. Hormonal problems (Cushing's disease is common in older dogs), diabetes and thyroid disease can cause increased appetite, which can lead to aggression related to food guarding. It's better to be proactive with your senior dog, making more frequent trips to the vet if necessary and having bloodwork done to test for the diseases that can commonly befall older dogs.

This is not to say that, as dogs age, they all fall apart physically and become nasty in personality. The aforementioned changes are discussed to alert owners to the things that may happen as their dogs get older. Many hardy dogs remain active and alert well into old age. However, it can be frustrating and heartbreaking for owners to see their beloved dogs change physically and temperamentally. Just know that it's the same Sussex under there, and that he still loves you and appreciates your care, which he needs now more than ever.

HOW DO I CARE FOR MY AGING DOG?

Again, every dog is an individual in terms of aging. Your dog might reach the estimated "senior" age and show no signs of slowing down. However, even if he shows no outward signs of aging, he should begin a senior-care program once he reaches the determined age. He may not show it, but he's not a pup anymore! By providing him with extra attention to his veterinary care at this age, you will be practicing good preventive medicine, ensuring that the rest of your dog's life will be as long, active, happy and healthy as possible. If you do notice indications of aging, such as graying and/or changes in sleeping, eating or toileting habits, this is a sign to set up a senior-care visit with your vet right away to make sure that these changes are not related to any health problems.

To start, senior dogs should visit the vet twice yearly for exams, routine tests and overall evaluations. Many veterinarians have special screening programs especially for senior dogs that can include a thorough physical exam; blood test to determine complete

WEATHER WORRIES

Older pets are less tolerant of extremes in weather, both heat and cold. Your older dog should not spend extended periods in the sun; when outdoors in the warm weather, make sure he does not become overheated. In chilly weather, consider a sweater for your dog when outdoors and limit time spent outside. Whether or not his coat is thinning, he will need provisions to keep him warm when the weather is cold. Make sure his bed or crate is in a draft-free area where he will not catch a chill.

blood count; serum biochemistry test, which screens for liver, kidney and blood problems as well as cancer; urinalysis; and dental exams. With these tests, it can be determined whether your dog has any health problems; the results also establish a baseline for your pet against which future test results can be compared.

In addition to these tests, your vet may suggest additional testing, including an EKG, tests for glaucoma and other problems of the eye, chest x-rays, screening for tumors, blood pressure test, test for thyroid function and screening for parasites and reassessment of his preventive program. Your vet also will ask you questions about your dog's diet and activity level, what you feed and the amounts that you feed. This information, along with his evaluation of the dog's overall condition, will enable him to suggest proper dietary changes, if needed.

This may seem like quite a work-up for your pet, but veterinarians advise that older dogs need more frequent attention so that any health problems can be detected as early as possible. Serious conditions like kidney disease, heart disease and cancer may not present outward symptoms, or the problem may go undetected if the symptoms are mistaken by owners as just part of the aging process.

There are some conditions more common in elderly dogs that are difficult to ignore. Cognitive dysfunction shares much in common with senility and Alzheimer's disease, and dogs are not immune. Dogs can become

AH, MY ACHING BONES!

As your pet ages and things that once were routine become difficult for him to handle, you may need to make some adjustments around the home to make things easier for your dog. Senior dogs affected by arthritis may have trouble moving about. If you notice this in your dog, you may have to limit him to one floor of the house so that he does not have to deal with stairs. If there are a few steps leading out into the yard, a ramp may help the dog. Likewise, he may need a ramp or a boost to get in and out of the car. Ensure that he has plenty of soft bedding on which to sleep and rest, as this will be comfortable for his aching joints. Also ensure that surfaces on which the dog walks are not slippery.

Investigate new dietary supplements made for arthritic dogs. Studies have found that products containing glucosamine added once or twice daily to the senior dog's food can have beneficial effects on the dog's joints. Many of these products also contain natural anti-inflammatories such as chondroitin, MSM and cetyl myristoleate, as well as natural herbal remedies and nutmeg. Talk to your vet about these supplements.

confused and/or disoriented, lose their house-training, have abnormal sleep-wake cycles and interact differently with their owners. Be heartened by the fact that, in some ways, there are more treatment options for dogs with cognitive dysfunction than for people with similar conditions. There is good evidence that continued stimulation in the form of games, play, training and exercise can help to maintain cognitive function. There are also medications (such as seligiline) and antioxidant-fortified senior diets that have been shown to be beneficial.

Cancer is also a condition more common in the elderly. Although lung cancer, which is a major killer in humans, is relatively rare in dogs, almost all of the cancers seen in people are also seen in pets. If pets are getting regular physical examinations, cancers are often detected early. There are a variety of cancer therapies available today, and many pets continue to live happy lives with appropriate treatment.

Degenerative joint disease, often referred to as arthritis, is another malady common to both elderly dogs and humans. A lifetime of wear and tear on joints and running around at play eventually takes its toll and results in stiffness and difficulty in getting around. As dogs live longer and healthier lives, it is natural that they should eventually feel some of the effects of aging. Once again, if regular veterinary care has been available, your pet should not have been carrying extra pounds all those years and wearing those joints out before their time. If your pet was unfortunate enough to inherit hip dysplasia, osteochondritis dissecans or any of the other developmental orthopedic diseases, battling the onset of degenerative joint disease was probably a long-standing goal. In any case, there are now many effective remedies for managing degenerative joint disease and a number of remarkable surgeries as well.

Aside from the extra veterinary care, there is much you can do at home to keep your older dog in good condition. The dog's diet is an important factor. If your dog's appetite decreases, he will not be getting the nutrients he needs. He also will lose weight,

WHAT A RELIEF!
Much like young puppies, older dogs do not have as much control over their excretory functions as they do as non-seniors. Their muscle control fades and, as such, they cannot "hold it" for as long as they used to. This is easily remedied by additional trips outside. If your dog's sight is failing, have the yard well lit at night and/or lead him to his relief site on lead. Incontinence should be discussed with your vet.

which is unhealthy for a dog at a proper weight. Conversely, an older dog's metabolism is slower and he usually exercises less, but he should not be allowed to become obese. Obesity in an older dog is especially risky, because extra pounds mean extra stress on the body, increasing his vulnerability to heart disease. Additionally, the extra pounds make it harder for the dog to move about.

You should discuss age-related feeding changes with your vet. For a dog who has lost interest in food, it may be suggested to try some different types of food until you find something new that the dog likes. For an obese dog, a "light"-formula dog food or reducing food portions may be advised, along with exercise appropriate to his physical condition and energy level.

As for exercise, the senior dog should not be allowed to become a "couch potato" despite his age. He may not be able to handle the morning run, long walks and vigorous games of fetch, but he still needs to get up and get moving. Keep up with your daily walks, but keep the distances shorter and let your dog set the pace. If he gets to the point where he's not up for walks, let him stroll around the yard. On the other hand, many dogs remain very active in their senior years, so base changes to the exercise program on your own individual dog and what he's capable of. Don't worry, your Sussex will let you know when it's time to rest.

Keep up with your grooming routine as you always have. Be extra diligent about checking the skin and coat for problems. Older dogs can experience thinning coats as a normal aging process, but they can also lose hair as a result of medical problems. Some thinning is normal, but patches of baldness or the loss of significant amounts of hair is not.

Hopefully, you've been regular with brushing your dog's teeth throughout his life. Healthy teeth directly affect overall good health. We already know that bacteria from gum infections can enter the dog's body through the damaged gums and travel to the organs. At a stage in life when his organs don't function as well as they used to, you don't want anything to put additional strain on them. Clean teeth also contribute to a healthy immune system. Offering the dental-type chews in addition to toothbrushing can help, as they remove plaque and tartar as the dog chews.

Along with the same good care you've given him all of his life, pay a little extra attention to your dog in his senior years and keep up with twice-yearly trips to the vet. The sooner a problem is uncovered, the greater the chances of a full recovery.

SHOWING YOUR

SUSSEX SPANIEL

Is dog showing in your blood? Are you excited by the idea of gaiting your handsome Sussex Spaniel around the ring to the thunderous applause of an enthusiastic audience? Are you certain that your beloved Sussex is flawless? You are not alone! Every loving owner thinks that his dog has no faults, or too few to mention. No matter how many times an owner reads the breed standard, he cannot find any faults in his aristocratic companion dog. If this sounds like you, and if you are considering entering your Sussex in a dog show, here are some basic questions to ask yourself:

- Did you purchase a "show-quality" puppy from the breeder?
- Is your puppy at least six months of age?
- Does the puppy exhibit correct show type for his breed?
- Does your puppy have any disqualifying faults?
- Is your Sussex registered with the American Kennel Club?
- How much time do you have to devote to training, grooming, conditioning and exhibiting your dog?

- Do you understand the rules and regulations of a dog show?
- Do you have time to learn how to show your dog properly?
- Do you have the financial resources to invest in showing your dog?
- Will you show the dog yourself or hire a professional handler?
- Do you have a vehicle that can accommodate your weekend trips to the dog shows?

Success in the show ring requires more than a pretty face, a waggy tail and a pocketful of liver. Even though dog shows can be exciting and enjoyable, the sport of conformation makes great demands on the exhibitors and the dogs. Winning exhibitors live for their dogs, devoting time and money to their dogs' presentation, conditioning and training. Very few novices, even those with good dogs, will find themselves in the winners' circle, though it does happen. Don't be disheartened, though. Every exhibitor began as a novice and worked his way up to the Group ring. It's the "working your way up" part that you must keep in mind.

Assuming that you have purchased a puppy of the correct type and quality for showing, let's begin to examine the world of showing and what's required to get started. Although the entry fee into a dog show is nominal, there are lots of other hidden costs involved with "finishing" your Sussex, that is, making him a champion. Things like equipment, travel, training and conditioning all cost money. A more serious campaign will include fees for a professional handler, boarding, cross-country travel and advertising. Top-winning show dogs can represent a very considerable investment—over $100,000 has been spent in campaigning some dogs. (The investment can be less, of course, for owners who don't use professional handlers.)

Many owners, on the other hand, enter their "average" Sussex in dog shows for the fun and enjoyment of it. Dog showing makes an absorbing hobby, with many rewards for dogs and owners alike. If you're having fun, meeting other people who share your interests and enjoying the overall experience, you likely will catch the "bug." Once the dog-show bug bites, its effects can last a lifetime; it's certainly much better than a deer tick! Soon you will be envisioning yourself in the center ring at the Westminster Kennel Club Dog Show in New York City, competing for the pres-tigious Best in Show cup. This magical dog show is televised annually from Madison Square

FOR MORE INFORMATION...

For reliable, up-to-date information about registration, dog shows and other canine competitions, contact one of the national registries by mail or via the Internet.

American Kennel Club
5580 Centerview Dr., Raleigh, NC 27606-3390
www.akc.org

United Kennel Club
100 E. Kilgore Road, Kalamazoo, MI 49002
www.ukcdogs.com

Canadian Kennel Club
89 Skyway Ave., Suite 100, Etobicoke, Ontario
M9W 6R4, Canada
www.ckc.ca

Garden, and the victorious dog becomes a celebrity overnight.

THE BASICS OF AKC CONFORMATION SHOWING

Visiting a dog show as a spectator is a great place to start. Pick up the show catalog to find out what time your breed is being shown, who is judging the breed and in which ring the classes will be held. To start, Sussex compete against other Sussex, and the winner is selected as Best of Breed by the judge. This is the procedure for each breed. At a group show, all of the Best of Breed winners go on to compete for Group One (first place) in their respective groups. For example, all Best of Breed winners in a given group compete against each other; this is done for all seven groups. Finally, all seven group winners go head to head in the

> **BECOMING A CHAMPION**
> An official AKC championship of record requires that a dog accumulate 15 points under 3 different judges, including 2 "majors" under different judges. Points are awarded based on the number of dogs entered into competition, varying from breed to breed and place to place. A win of three, four or five points is considered a "major." The AKC annually assigns a schedule of points to adjust for variations that accompany a breed's popularity and the population of a given area.

ring for the Best in Show award.

What most spectators don't understand is the basic idea of conformation. A dog show is often referred to as a "conformation" show. This means that the judge should decide how each dog stacks up (conforms) to the breed standard for his given breed: how well does this Sussex Spaniel conform to the ideal representative detailed in the standard? Ideally, this is what happens. In reality, however, this ideal often gets slighted as the judge compares Sussex #1 to Sussex #2. Again, the ideal is that each dog is judged based on his merits in comparison to his breed standard, not in comparison to the other dogs in the ring. It is easier for judges to compare dogs of the same breed to decide which they think is the

Ch. Companionwy Brighton's Stones is shown winning Best in Show at Merrimack Valley Kennel Club under judge Robert Caswell.

better specimen; in the Group and Best in Show ring, however, it is very difficult to compare one breed to another, like apples to oranges. Thus the dog's conformation to the breed standard—not to mention advertising dollars and good handling—is essential to success in conformation shows. The dog described in the standard (the standard for each AKC breed is written and approved by the breed's national parent club and then submitted to the AKC for approval) is the perfect dog of that breed, and breeders keep their eye on the standard when they choose

Ch. Clussexx Harry Potter TD wins the Sporting Group at the Hoosier Kennel Club.

> ## FIVE CLASSES AT SHOWS
> At most AKC all-breed shows, there are five regular classes offered: Puppy, Novice, Bred-by-Exhibitor, American-bred and Open. The Puppy Class is usually divided as 6 to 12 months of age and 12 to 18 months of age. When deciding in which class to enter your dog, whether male or female, you must carefully check the show schedule to make sure that you have selected the right class. Depending on the age of the dog, previous first-place wins and the sex of the dog, you must make the best choice. It is possible to enter a one-year-old dog who has not won sufficient first places in any of the non-Puppy Classes, though the competition is more intense the further you progress from the Puppy Class.

---

which dogs to breed, hoping to get closer and closer to the ideal with each litter.

Another good first step for the novice is to join a dog club. You will be astonished by the many and different kinds of dog clubs in the country, with about 5,000 clubs holding events every year. Most clubs require that prospective new members present two letters of recommendation from existing members. Perhaps you've made some friends visiting a show held by a particular club and you would like to join that club. Dog clubs may specialize in a single breed, like a local or regional Sussex club, or in a specific pursuit, such as obedience, tracking or hunting tests. There are all-breed clubs for all dog enthusiasts; they sponsor special training days, seminars on

At benched shows, dogs wait in designated areas, usually grouped by breed, until their time in the ring.

At benched shows, dogs wait in designated areas, usually grouped by breed, until their time in the ring.

topics like grooming or handling or lectures on breeding or canine genetics. There are also clubs that specialize in certain types of dogs, like hunting dogs, spaniel breeds, companion dogs, etc.

A parent club is the national organization, sanctioned by the AKC, which promotes and safe-guards its breed in the country. The Sussex Spaniel Club of America was formed in 1981, just over a decade after the breed was re-established in the US. The club can be contacted on the Internet at www.sussexspaniels.org. The parent club holds an annual national specialty show, usually in a different city each year, in which many of the country's top dogs, handlers and breeders gather to compete. At a specialty show, only members of a single breed are invited to participate.

There are also group specialties, in which all members of a group are invited. For more information about dog clubs in your area, contact the AKC at www.akc.org on the Internet or write them at their Raleigh, NC address.

OTHER TYPES OF COMPETITION

In addition to conformation shows, the AKC holds a variety of other competitive events. Obedience trials, agility trials and tracking trials are open to all breeds, while hunting tests, field trials, lure coursing, herding tests and trials, earthdog tests and coonhound events are limited to specific breeds or groups of breeds. The Junior Showmanship Program is offered to aspiring young handlers and their dogs, and the Canine Good Citizen® Program is an all-around good-behavior test open to all dogs, pure-bred and mixed.

OBEDIENCE TRIALS

There are three levels of difficulty in obedience competition. The

---

THE VERSATILE SUSSEX

The Sussex Spaniel Club of America offers a club Versatility Award, which recognizes Sussex who have earned an AKC championship title, a hunting title and an obedience, tracking or agility title.

first (and easiest) level is the Novice, in which dogs can earn the Companion Dog (CD) title. The intermediate level is the Open level, in which the Companion Dog Excellent (CDX) title is awarded. The advanced level is the Utility level, in which dogs compete for the Utility Dog (UD) title. Classes at each level are further divided into "A" and "B," with "A" for beginners and "B" for those with more experience. In order to win a title at a given level, a dog must earn three "legs." A "leg" is accomplished when a dog scores 170 or higher (200 is a perfect score). The scoring system gets a little trickier when you understand that a dog must score more than 50% of the points available for each exercise in order to actually earn the points. Available points for each exercise range between 20 and 40.

A dog must complete different exercises at each level of obedience. The Novice exercises are the easiest, with the Open and finally the Utility levels progressing in difficulty. Examples of Novice exercises are on- and off-lead heeling, a figure-8 pattern, performing a recall (or come), long sit and long down and standing for examination. In the Open level, the Novice-level exercises are required again, but this time without a leash and for longer durations. In addition, the dog must clear a broad jump, retrieve over a jump and drop on

recall. In the Utility level, the exercises are quite difficult, including executing basic commands based on hand signals, following a complex heeling pattern, locating articles based on scent discrimination and completing jumps at the handler's direction. The first Sussex Spaniel to earn the Utility Dog title was Resolute Hudson of Askonandy UD.

Once he's earned the UD title, a dog can go on to win the prestigious title of Utility Dog Excellent (UDX) by winning "legs" in ten shows. Additionally, Utility Dogs who win "legs" in Open B and Utility B earn points toward the lofty title of Obedience Trial Champion (OTCh.). Established in 1977 by the AKC, this title requires a dog to earn 100 points as well as 3 first places in a combination of Open B and Utility B classes under 3 different judges. The "brass ring" of obedience competition is the AKC's National Obedience Invitational. This is an exclusive competition for only the cream of the obedi-

The judge assesses the line of Sussex in the breed ring, not comparing the dogs against each other but rather deciding which of the competitors most closely matches the ideal set forth in the breed standard.

ence crop. In order to qualify for the invitational, a dog must be ranked in either the top 25 all-breeds in obedience or in the top 3 for his breed in obedience. The title at stake here is that of National Obedience Champion (NOC).

RALLY OBEDIENCE

In 2005 the AKC began a new program called rally obedience, and soon this exciting obedience spin-off began sweeping the US. This is a less formal activity in which titles are awarded. There are four levels of competition: Novice, Advanced, Excellent and Advanced/Excellent. The dog and handler do a series of exercises designated by the judge and are timed. The judge evaluates each team on how well it executes one continuous performance over the

The judge examines each dog physically to ensure the presence of correct bone structure and bite, traits that cannot be sufficiently evaluated simply by looking at the dog.

CANINE GOOD CITIZEN® PROGRAM

Have you ever considered getting your dog "certified"? The AKC's Canine Good Citizen® Program affords your dog just that opportunity. Your dog shows that he is a well-behaved canine citizen, using the basic training and good manners you have taught him, by taking a series of ten tests that illustrate that he can behave properly at home, in a public place and around other dogs. The tests are administered by participating dog clubs, colleges, 4-H clubs, Scouts and other community groups and are open to all pure-bred and mixed-breed dogs. Upon passing the ten tests, the suffix CGC is then applied to your dog's name.

The ten tests are: 1. Accepting a friendly stranger; 2. Sitting politely for petting; 3. Appearance and grooming; 4. Walking on a lead; 5. Walking through a group of people; 6. Sit, down and stay on command; 7. Coming when called; 8. Meeting another dog; 9. Calm reaction to distractions; 10. Separation from owner.

whole course.

The team works on its own as soon as the judge gives the order to begin. The handlers are encouraged to talk to their dog as they work through the course. Handlers develop their own style in working with their dogs, using a combination of body language and hand signals as well as verbal commands. Faster and more accurate performances are desirable, though each team must work at its own pace. Signs are set up around the ring to indicate which exercise (or combination of exercises) is required. Working closely around the course, the team heels from one sign to the next, performing between 10 and 20 exercises. There are 50 exercises to choose from, varying in complexity and difficulty.

The dogs love this event and it shows by their animation and energy. Many of the dogs who participate in obedience or agility also do well in rally. While most of the first rally titles have gone to seasoned obedience dogs, it's encouraging that some newcomers have also earned awards. Rally is a good way for a beginner to start out in obedience, and we hope that it will become a stepping

The FCI governs most shows on the Continent. This photo was taken at a show in the Netherlands.

stone to the obedience world and we will see many more dogs and owners coming into the ring.

AGILITY TRIALS

Agility trials became sanctioned by the AKC in August 1994, when the first licensed agility trials were held. Since that time, agility certainly has grown in popularity by leaps and bounds, literally! The AKC allows all registered breeds (including Miscellaneous Class breeds) to participate, providing the dog is 12 months of age or older. Agility is designed so that the handler demonstrates how well the dog can work at his side. The handler directs his dog through, over, under and around an obstacle course that includes jumps, tires, the dog walk, weave poles, pipe tunnels, collapsed tunnels and more. While working his way through the course, the

TALENTED TRACKER

An area of the dog sport for which the Sussex Spaniel is ideally suited is tracking. This a sport that comes naturally, and the Sussex excels in using his superior nose. Contact a Sussex Spaniel club for information on how you can become involved in tracking events, whether for competition or just for fun, with your Sussex.

FIRST MASTER HUNTER

In 2003, Ch. Sundowner Swing That Music MH, fondly kown as "Satch," became the first Sussex Spaniel to earn the Master Hunter (MH) title. Satch is owned by Jan Hepper and was trained and handled to his MH title by Don Krueger.

age. The USDAA and AKC both offer titles to winning dogs, although the exercises and requirements of the two organizations differ. Sussex Spaniels have demonstrated superior ability in competitive agility in the United States but have not been seen much in agility in other countries.

Agility trials are a great way to keep your dog active, and they will keep you running, too! You should join a local agility club to learn more about the sport. These clubs offer sessions in which you can introduce your dog to the various obstacles as well as training classes to prepare him for competition. In no time, your dog will be climbing A-frames, crossing the dog walk and flying over hurdles, all with you right beside him. Your heart will leap every time your dog jumps through the hoop—and you'll be having just as much (if not more) fun!

HUNTING TESTS

Hunting tests are not competitive like field trials, and participating dogs are judged against a standard, as in a conformation show. The first hunting tests were devised by the North American Hunting Retriever Association (NAHRA) as an alternative to field trials for retriever owners to appreciate their dogs' natural innate ability in the field without the expense and pressure of a formal field trial. The intent of

dog must keep one eye and ear on the handler and the rest of his body on the course. The handler runs along with the dog, giving verbal and hand signals to guide the dog through the course.

The first organization to promote agility trials in the US was the United States Dog Agility Association, Inc. (USDAA). Established in 1986, the USDAA sparked the formation of many member clubs around the country. To participate in USDAA trials, dogs must be at least 18 months of

COMPETITIVE FIELD WORK

In the US, Sussex Spaniels are ineligible for interbreed competition such as field trials but are eligible to run with other spaniel breeds to attain criterion-based hunt titles. In the UK, Sussex Spaniels have a longer history of working in the field, actually competing successfully in trials before World War II, and have truly begun to hold their own in fieldwork when competing against other rare spaniel breeds such as the Welsh Springer Spaniel and Clumber Spaniel.

had no split between working and show types. The same Sussex who can win at a dog show can also perform well in the field, provided the proper training has been done to introduce the dog to field work. The Sussex Spaniel is built low to the ground and thus hunts at a slower pace than the English Springer Spaniel. He is methodical and determined and with his slower pace may be a better fit for many hunters as he does not speed through the cover, but rather deliberately works it. Once the scent of a bird is discovered, the Sussex tail wags faster and faster as he hones in on the scent. Upon reaching a bird, the Sussex will move in to perform a deliberate flush. The Sussex Spaniel Club of America hosts spaniel hunt tests, working dog tests and fun field training events. Sussex Spaniels are not eligible to run in field trials in the US.

hunting tests is the same as that of field trials: to test the dog's ability in a simulated hunting scenario.

The AKC instituted its hunting tests in June 1985; since then, their popularity has grown tremendously. The AKC offers three titles at hunting tests, Junior Hunter (JH), Senior Hunter (SH) and Master Hunter (MH). Each title requires that the dog earn qualifying "legs" at the tests: the JH requiring four; the SH, five; and the MH, six. In addition to the AKC, the United Kennel Club also offers hunting tests through its affiliate club, the Hunting Retriever Club, Inc. (HRC), which began the tests in 1984.

Unlike some other spaniel breeds, the Sussex Spaniel has

A treat in the ring gets the dog to stand at attention and look his best.

SUSSEX SPANIEL

You chose your dog because something clicked the minute you set eyes on him. Or perhaps it seemed that the dog selected you and that's what clinched the deal. Either way, you are now investing time and money in this dog, a true pal and an outstanding member of the family. Everything about him is perfect—well, almost perfect. Remember, he is a dog! For that matter, how does he think *you're* doing?

UNDERSTANDING THE CANINE MINDSET

For starters, you and your dog are on different wavelengths. Your dog is similar to a toddler in that both live in the present tense only. A dog's view of life is based primarily on cause and effect; your dog makes connections based on the fact that he lives in the present, so when he is doing something and you interrupt to dispense praise or a correction, a connection, positive or negative, is made. To the dog, that's like one plus one equals two! In the same sense, it's also easy to see that when your timing is off, you will cause an incorrect connection.

The one-plus-one way of thinking is why you must never scold a dog for behavior that took place an hour, 15 minutes or even 5 seconds ago. But it is also why, when your timing is perfect, you can teach him to do all kinds of wonderful things—as soon as he has made that essential connection. What helps the process is his desire to please you and to have your approval.

There are behaviors we admire in dogs, such as friendliness and obedience, as well as those behaviors that cause problems to a varying degree. The dog owner who encounters minor behavioral problems is wise to solve them promptly or get professional help. Bad behaviors are not corrected by repeatedly shouting "No" or getting angry with the dog. Only the giving of praise and approval for good behavior lets your dog understand right from wrong. The longer a bad behavior is allowed to continue, the harder it is to overcome. A responsible breeder is often able to help. Each dog is unique, so try not to compare your dog's behavior with your neighbor's dog or the one you had as a child.

Have your veterinarian check the dog to see whether a behavior problem could have a physical cause. An earache or toothache, for example, could be the reason for a dog to snap at you if you were to touch his head when putting on his leash. A sharp correction from you would only increase the behavior. When a physical basis is eliminated, and if the problem is not something you understand or can cope with, ask for the name of a behavioral specialist, preferably one who is familiar with the Sussex. Be sure to keep the breeder informed of your progress.

Many things, such as environment and inherited traits, form the basic behavior of a dog, just as in humans. You also must factor into his temperament the purpose for which your dog was originally bred. The major obstacle lies in the dog's inability to explain his behavior to us in a way that we understand. The one thing you should not do is to give up and abandon your dog. Somewhere a misunderstanding has occurred but, with help and patient understanding on your part, you should be able to work out the majority of bothersome behaviors.

AGGRESSION

The Sussex Spaniel should not be an aggressive breed; in fact, the breed standard states that he

Sussex Spaniels should be non-aggressive by nature, including toward other dogs, although this needs to be nurtured by careful introduction and socialization.

should be "friendly" and "cheerful." The British standard even states that aggression is "highly undesirable." Nonetheless, aggression is a problem that concerns all responsible dog owners since, when not controlled, aggression always becomes dangerous. An aggressive dog, no matter the size, may lunge at, bite or even attack a person or another dog.

Aggressive behavior is not to be tolerated. It is more than just inappropriate behavior; it is painful for a family to watch their dog become unpredictable in his behavior to the point where they are afraid of him. While not all aggressive behavior is dangerous, growling, baring teeth, etc., can be frightening. It is important to ascertain why the dog is acting in this manner. Aggression is a display of dominance, and the dog should not have the dominant role in his pack, which is, in this case, your family.

Sussex Spaniels are often possessive of their owners, which

may be misinterpreted as aggression. A Sussex may live happily with other dogs, provided they are trained and socialized to do so. However, the Sussex prefers to be the "top dog" and care should be taken in introducing another dog to the household. Disputes can arise over "possessions," be it a favored toy or even the owner himself. It cannot be said enough that early socialization plays a large role in avoiding aggressive behavior.

If a Sussex exhibits aggressive tendencies, behavior modification techniques should be used. Interventions must rely on techniques that avoid overly corrective maneuvers. It is just good sense that corrective measures that are physical in nature may be seen as aggressive by a dog of any breed. This increases the likelihood that the dog will respond aggressively. In this scenario, the aggression escalates.

It is important not to challenge an aggressive dog, as this could provoke an attack. Observe your Sussex Spaniel's body language. Does he make direct eye contact and stare? Does he try to make himself as large as possible: ears pricked, chest out, tail erect? Height and size signify authority in a dog pack—being taller or "above" another dog literally means that he is "above" in social status. These body signals tell you that your Sussex Spaniel thinks

he is in charge, a problem that needs to be addressed. An aggressive dog is unpredictable; you never know when he is going to strike and what he is going to do. You cannot understand why a dog that is playful one minute is growling the next.

Fear is a common cause of aggression in dogs. Perhaps your Sussex Spaniel had a negative experience as a puppy, which causes him to be fearful when a similar situation presents itself later in life. The dog may act aggressively in order to protect himself from whatever is making him afraid. It is not always easy to determine what is making your dog fearful, but if you can isolate what brings out the fear reaction, you can help the dog overcome it.

Supervise your Sussex Spaniel's interactions with people and other dogs, and praise the dog

FEAR BITING

The remedy for the fear biter is in the hands of a professional trainer or behaviorist. This is not a behavior that the average pet owner should attempt to correct. However, there are things you should not do. Don't sympathize with him, don't pet him and don't, whatever you do, pick him up—you could be bitten in the process, which is even scarier if you bring him up near your face.

when it goes well. If he starts to act aggressively in a situation, correct him and remove him from the situation. Do not let people approach the dog and start petting him without your express permission. That way, you can have the dog sit to accept petting, and praise him when he behaves properly. You are focusing on praise and on modifying his behavior by rewarding him when he acts appropriately. By being gentle and by supervising his interactions, you are showing him that there is no need to be afraid or defensive.

The best solution is to consult a behavioral specialist, one who has experience with the breed or at least with spaniels. Together, you can try to pinpoint the cause of your dog's aggression and do something about it.

SEPARATION ANXIETY

Sussex Spaniels can be intensely involved in the daily lives of their human pack. They are not a "go lie down and leave me alone" kind of dog. Sussex Spaniels actively seek human companionship and generally will work hard to get it. The breed must have significant daily human interaction to be at its best.

Any behaviorist will tell you that separation anxiety is the most common problem about which pet owners complain. It is also one of the easiest to prevent. Unfortunately, a behaviorist

I CAN'T SMILE WITHOUT YOU

How can you tell whether your dog is suffering from separation anxiety? Not every dog who enjoys a close bond with his owner will suffer from separation anxiety. In actuality, only a small percentage of dogs are affected. Separation anxiety manifests itself in dogs older than one year of age and may not occur until the dog is a senior. A number of destructive behaviors are associated with the problem, including scratch marks in front of doorways, bite marks on furniture, drool stains on furniture and flooring and tattered draperies, carpets or cushions. The most reliable sign of separation anxiety is howling and crying when the owner leaves and then barking like mad for extended periods. Affected dogs may also defecate or urinate throughout the home, attempt to escape when the door opens, vocalize excessively and show signs of depression (including loss of appetite, listlessness and lack of activity).

I GOTTA RIGHT TO SING THE BLUES

The term "separation anxiety" resonates with modern-day "psychobabble" overtones and therefore may be shunned by dog owners as an imaginary New Age disorder. On the contrary, veterinary behaviorists have begun to treat the condition like a real problem. Recently some drug therapies that have shown positive effects on dogs who suffer from separation anxiety have entered the market; among the most successful are Prozac® and Clomicalm®.

If anti-anxiety drugs don't work, consider getting your canine pal a pal of his own. Introducing a second dog to the household may do wonders for your dog's spirits. For dog owners who must be out of the house for eight or more hours a day for work, a second dog is an excellent choice. Another option is to hire a dog walker or dog sitter so that your dog isn't alone for long periods of time. There are also doggie day-care centers that offer reliable services at reasonable prices. Check your phone book for listings or take a look online for facilities in your area. More and more dog owners use their services, so ask around to get recommendations.

usually is not consulted until the dog is a stressed-out, neurotic mess. At that stage, it is indeed a problem that requires the help of a professional.

Training the puppy to the fact that people in the house come and go is essential in order to avoid this anxiety. Leaving the puppy in his crate or a confined area while family members go in and out, and stay out for longer and longer periods of time, is the basic way to desensitize the pup to the family's frequent departures. If you are at home most of every day, make it a point to go out for at least an hour or two whenever possible.

How you leave is vital to the dog's reaction. Your dog is no fool. He knows the difference between sweats and business suits, jeans and dresses. He sees you pat your pocket to check for your wallet, open your briefcase, check that you have your cell phone or pick up the car keys. He knows from the hurry of the kids in the morning that they're off to school until afternoon. Lipstick? Aftershave lotion? Lunch boxes? Every move you make registers in his sensory perception and memory. Your puppy knows more about your departures than you do. You can't get away with a thing!

Before you got dressed, you checked the dog's water bowl and his supply of long-lasting chew toys and you turned the radio on low. You will leave him in what he considers his "safe" area, not with total freedom of the house. If you've invested in child safety gates, you can be reasonably sure that he'll remain in the designated area. Don't give him access to a window where he can watch you leave the house. If you're leaving for an hour or two, just put him into his crate with a safe toy.

Now comes the test! You are ready to walk out the door. Do not give your Sussex a big hug and a fond farewell. Do not drag out a long goodbye. Those are the very things that jump-start separation anxiety. Toss a biscuit into the dog's area, call out "So long, pooch" and close the door. You're gone. The chances are that the dog may bark a couple of times, or maybe whine once or twice, and then settle down to enjoy his biscuit and take a lovely nap, especially if you took him for a nice long walk after breakfast. As he grows up, the barks and whines will stop because it's an old routine, so why should he make the effort?

DOMINANCE

Dogs are born with dominance skills, meaning that they can be quite clever in trying to get their way. The "follow-me" trot to the cookie jar is an example. The toy dropped in your lap says "Play with me." The leash delivered to you along with an excited look means "Take me for a walk." These are all good-natured dominant behaviors. Ask your dog to sit before agreeing to his request and you'll remain "top dog."

When you first brought home the puppy, the come-and-go routine was intermittent and constant. He was put into his crate with a tiny treat. You left (silently) and returned in 3 minutes, then 5, then 10, then 15, then half an hour, until finally you could leave without a problem and be gone for 2 or 3 hours. If, at any time in the future, there's a "separation" problem, refresh his memory by going back to that basic training.

Now comes the next most important part—your return. Do not make a big production of coming home. "Hi, poochie" is as grand a greeting as he needs. When you've taken off your hat and coat, tossed your briefcase on the hall table and glanced at the mail, and the dog has settled down from the excitement of seeing you "in person" from his confined area, then go and give him a warm, friendly greeting. A

The Sussex is loyal and affectionate, thriving on attention from his owner. Be sure to spend time with your Sussex if you are out of the house all day—let him know that he is a valued member of the family!

potty trip is needed and a walk would be appreciated, since he's been such a good dog.

MATTERS OF SEX

For whatever reasons, real or imagined, most people tend to have a preference in choosing between a male and female puppy. Some, but not all, of the undesirable traits attributed to the sex of the dog can be suppressed by early spaying or neutering. The major advantage, of course, is that a neutered male or a spayed female will not be adding to the overpopulation of dogs.

An unaltered male will mark territory by lifting his leg everywhere, leaving a few drops of urine indoors on your furniture and appliances and outside on everything he passes. It is difficult to catch him in the act, because he leaves only a few drops each time, but it is very hard to eliminate the odor. Thus the cycle begins, because the odor will entice him to mark that spot again.

If you have bought a bitch with the intention of breeding her, be sure you know what you are getting into. She will go through one or two periods of estrus each year, each cycle lasting about three weeks. During those times she will have to be kept confined to protect your furniture and to protect her from being bred by a male other than the one you have selected. Breeding should never be under-

taken to "show the kids the miracle of birth." Bitches can die giving birth, and the puppies may also die. The dam often exhibits what is called "maternal aggression" after the pups are born. Her intention is to protect her pups, but in fact she can be extremely vicious. Breeding should be left to the experienced breeders, who do so for the betterment of the breed and with much research and planning behind each mating.

Mounting is not unusual in dogs, male or female. Puppies do it to each other and adults do it regardless of sex, because it is not so much a sexual act as it is one of dominance. It becomes very annoying when the dog mounts your legs, the kids or the couch cushions; in these and any other instances of mounting, he should be corrected. Touching sometimes stimulates the dog, so pulling the dog off by his collar or leash, together with a consistent and stern "Off!" command, usually eliminates the behavior.

GET A WHIFF OF HIM!
Dogs sniff each others' rears as their way of saying "Hi" as well as to find out who the other dog is and how he's doing. That's normal behavior between canines, but it can, annoyingly, extend to people. The command for all unwanted sniffing is "Leave it!" Give the command in a no-nonsense voice and move on.

CHEWING

All puppies chew. All dogs chew. This is a fact of life for canines, and sometimes you may think it's what your dog does best! A pup starts chewing when his first set of teeth erupts and continues throughout the teething period. Chewing gives the pup relief from itchy gums and incoming teeth and, from that time on, he gets great satisfaction out of this normal, somewhat idle, canine activity. Providing safe chew toys is the best way to direct this behavior in an appropriate manner. Chew toys are available in all sizes, textures and flavors, but you must monitor the wear-and-tear inflicted on your pup's toys to be sure that the ones you've chosen are safe and remain in good condition.

Sussex Spaniels are known to resort to chewing to entertain themselves if bored. Be an informed owner and purchase proper chew toys, like strong nylon bones, that will not splinter. Be sure that the objects are safe and durable, since your dog's safety is at risk. Again, the owner is responsible for ensuring a dog-proof environment. Items like rawhide, chew hooves and the like are not recommended. They can become messy and destroyed in no time and have been known to result in digestive ailments, sometimes requiring surgery.

Puppies cannot distinguish

> ## "DOG" SPOKEN HERE
> Dogs' verbal language is limited to four words: growl, bark, whine and howl. Their body language is what tells the tale. They communicate with each other, and hopefully with you, through precise postures. You know what the friendly wagging tail and the play-bow (down in front, up in rear) mean, but there's many other things that you can decipher from your dog's body language. When the dog turns belly up, or on his side with one leg raised, he's being totally submissive. Looking away (breaking eye contact) and laid-back ears are other signs of submission. With ears at attention, mouth open and tail in a neutral position, the dog is watchful but relaxed. Fear is indicated by a crouching, even trembling, posture, with ears back, tail down and eyes averted. The aggressive dog attempts to look as large as possible to his adversary. He stalks stiffly, with his tail up, head high, ears alert, hackles raised, chest puffed out and lips curled, and with a stare that is cold and hard.

between certain chew toys and a nice leather shoe or wallet. It's up to you to keep your possessions away from the dog and to keep your eye on the dog. There's a form of destruction caused by chewing that is not the dog's fault. Let's say you allow him on the sofa. One day he takes a toy up on

Digging is a natural instinct for most dogs, though you may not appreciate your Sussex's gardening talents. While difficult to stop entirely, digging behavior can be modified and controlled for good behavior and safety.

the sofa and, in the course of chewing on it, takes up a bit of fabric. He continues to chew. Disaster! Now you've learned the lesson: dogs with chew toys have to be either kept off furniture and carpets, carefully supervised or put into their confined areas for chew time.

The wooden legs of furniture are favorite objects for chewing. The first time, tell the dog "Leave it!" (or "No!") and offer him a chew toy as a substitute. But your clever dog may be hiding under the chair and doing some silent destruction, which you may not notice until it's too late. In this case, it's time to try one of the foul-tasting products, made specifically to prevent destructive chewing, that is sprayed on the objects of your

dog's chewing attention. These products also work to keep the dog away from plants, trash, etc. It's even a good way to stop the dog from "mouthing" or chewing on your hands or the leg of your pants. (Be sure to wash your hands after the mouthing lesson!) A little spray goes a long way.

DIGGING

Digging, which is seen as a destructive behavior to humans, is actually quite a natural behavior in dogs. Although terriers (the "earth dogs") are most associated with the digging, any dog's desire to dig can be irrepressible and most frustrating to his owners. When digging occurs in your yard, it is actually a normal behavior redirected into something the dog can do in his every-day life. In the wild, a dog would be actively seeking food, making his own shelter, etc. He would be using his paws in a purposeful manner for his survival. Since you provide him with food and shelter, he has no need to use his paws for these purposes, and so the energy that he would be using may manifest itself in the form of little holes all over your yard and flower beds.

Sussex Spaniels are notorious problem solvers, which means that they may turn their digging talents into "solving the problem" of confinement in the fenced yard. For this reason, fences must be embedded securely into the ground at a depth of at least one foot, and fences must be kept in good repair. Inspect the fence regularly to check for evidence of an escape artist at work, and secure any gaps or holes.

Perhaps your Sussex is digging as a reaction to boredom—it is somewhat similar to someone eating a whole bag of chips in front of the TV—because they are there and there is nothing better to do! Basically, the answer is to provide the dog with adequate play and exercise so that his mind and paws are occupied, and so that he feels as if he is doing something useful.

Of course, digging is easiest to control if it is stopped as soon as possible, but it is often hard to

catch a dog in the act. If your dog is a compulsive digger and is not easily distracted by other activities, you can designate a safe area on your property where he is allowed to dig. If you catch him digging in an off-limits area of the yard, immediately bring him to the approved area and praise him for digging there. Keep a close eye on him so that you can catch him in the act—that is the only way to make him understand what is permitted and what is not. If you take him to a hole he dug an hour

CUT TO THE CHASE

Chasing small animals is in the blood of many dogs, perhaps most; they think that this is a fun recreational activity (although some are more likely to bring you an undesirable "gift" as a result of the hunt). The good old "Leave it" command works to deter your dog from taking off in pursuit of "prey" but only if taught with the dog on leash for control.

Chasing cars or bikes is dangerous for all parties concerned: dogs, drivers and cyclists. Something about those wheels going around fascinates dogs, but that fascination can end in disastrous results. Corrections for your dog's chasing behavior must be immediate and firm. Tell him "Leave it!" and then give him either a sit or a down command. Get kids on bikes to help saturate your dog with spinning wheels while he politely practices his sits and downs.

ago and tell him "No," he will understand that you are not fond of holes, dirt or flowers. If you catch him while he is stifle-deep in your tulips, that is when he will get your message.

BARKING

Dogs cannot talk—oh, what they would say if they could! Instead, barking is a dog's way of "talking." It can be somewhat frustrating because it is not always easy to tell what a dog means by his bark—is he excited, happy, frightened or angry? Whatever it is that the dog is trying to say, he should not be punished for barking. It is only when the barking becomes excessive, and when the excessive barking becomes a bad habit, that the behavior needs to be modified.

Some Sussex Spaniels are quite vocal, using their barks to alert owners of suspicious noises and such. Many Sussex Spaniels express their enthusiasm for an activity, such as being released from a crate for training or work, with brief, happy barks or yips. They are also vocally responsive to owners who elicit the comical Sussex snort and barking as part of play and other interactions. The Sussex's vocalizations are expressive and range from yips and yodels to barks and howls. Fanciers report that a household with more than one Sussex may have a vocal chorus, as howling in unison is not unknown.

The Sussex Spaniel's vocalizations are a unique trait of the breed and should not be discouraged unless they become habitual and excessive. This is a problem that should be corrected early on. Sussex Spaniels must be taught when it is appropriate to use their expressive voices; teaching a "quiet" command is highly recommended.

As your Sussex Spaniel grows up, you will be able to tell when his barking is purposeful and when it is for no reason. You will become able to distinguish your dog's different barks and their meanings. For example, the bark when someone comes to the door will be different from the bark

STORM WARNING

Dogs sense approaching storms by barometric pressure changes. Many dogs do not like storms and head for cover under the bed, in a corner, in a closet, under a table, wherever they feel safe. To desensitize your dog to storms and to show him that he has nothing to fear, buy an audiotape of thunderstorm sounds. Set it so that you can barely hear it and sit in a closed room, where you'll read the paper while your dog listens to his new "storm" toy. Turn it off after a few fearless minutes. Repeat, increasing the sound level only as the dog tolerates it.

when he is excited to see you. It is similar to a person's tone of voice, except that the dog has to rely totally on tone of voice because he does not have the benefit of using words. An incessant barker will be evident at an early age.

There are some things that encourage a dog to bark. For example, if your dog barks non-stop for a few minutes and you give him a treat to quiet him, he believes that you are rewarding him for barking. He will associate barking with getting a treat and will keep doing it until he is rewarded. On the other hand, if you give him a command such as "Quiet" and praise him after he has stopped barking for a few seconds, he will get the idea that being "quiet" is what you want him to do.

FOOD-RELATED PROBLEMS

We're not talking about eating, diets or nutrition here, we're talking about bad habits. Face it. All dogs are beggars. Food is the motivation for everything we want our dogs to do and, when you combine that with their innate ability to "con" us in order to get their way, it's a wonder there aren't far more obese dogs in the world.

Who can resist the bleeding-heart look that says "I'm starving," the paw that gently pats your knee, along with a knowing

The Sussex Spaniel is a wonderful companion—loyal, affectionate and packed with personality.

look, the whining "please" or even the total body language of a perfect sit beneath the cookie jar. No one who professes to love his dog can turn down the pleas of his clever canine's performances every time. One thing is for sure, though: definitely do not allow begging at the table. Family meals do not include your dog.

Control your dog's begging habit by making your dog work for his rewards. Ignore his begging when you can. Utilize the obedience commands you've taught your dog. Use "Off" for the pawing. A sit or even a long down will interrupt the whining. His reward in these situations is definitely not a treat. Casual verbal praise is enough. Be sure all members of the family follow the same rules.

There is a different type of begging that does demand your

immediate response and that is the appeal to be let (or taken) outside! Usually that is a quick paw or small whine to get your attention, followed by a race to the door. This type of begging needs your quick attention and approval. Of course, a really smart dog will soon figure out how to cut you off at the pass and direct you to that cookie jar on your way to the door! Some dogs are always one step ahead of us.

Stealing food is a problem only if you are not paying attention. A dog can't steal food that is not within his reach. Leaving your dog in the kitchen with the roast beef on the table is asking for trouble. Putting cheese and crackers on the coffee table also requires a watchful eye to stop the thief in his tracks. The word to use (one word, remember, even if it's two words pronounced as one) is "Leave it!" Instead of preceding it with yet another "No," try using a guttural sound like "Aagh!" That sounds more like a warning growl to the dog and therefore has instant meaning.

Canine thieves are in their element when little kids are carrying cookies in their hands. Your dog will think he's been excep-

PANHANDLING POOCHES

If there's one thing at which dogs excel, it is begging. If there's one thing that owners lack, it's the willpower to resist giving in to their canine beggars! If you don't give in to your adorable puppy, he won't grow into an adult dog that's a nuisance. However, give in just once and the dog will forever figure, "maybe this time." Treats are rewards for correct performance, a category into which begging definitely does not fall.

tionally clever if he causes a child to drop a cookie. Bonanza! The easiest solution is to keep dog and children separated at snack time. You must also be sure that the children understand that they must not tease the dog with food—his or theirs. Your dog does not mean to bite the kids, but when he snatches at a tidbit so near the level of his mouth, it can result in an unintended nip.

EATING EXCREMENT

The unpleasant subject of dogs' eating their own feces, known as coprophagia, can be dealt with relatively easily even though no one is exactly sure why dogs do this. Some say it is primordial, while others feel that it indicates a lack of something in the diet (but there's no agreement as to what that "something" is). Unless the dog has worms, feces eating cannot make him sick, but that is no reason to allow it to continue. There are products said to alleviate the problem, but check with your vet before adding anything to your puppy's diet. Sprinkling hot pepper on the feces is an after-the-fact solution. Prevention is the better way to go.

When you house-trained your dog, you took him outside on a leash and stayed with him until he did his business. Afterward, you moved him away or took him back indoors while you went back and cleaned up the feces. You were not giving him any opportunity to indulge in this strange canine habit. Now that your dog goes outside alone, watch to see that it doesn't start. At his first sign of interest in his own excrement, or that of any other animal, give him a sharp "No! Leave it!" and then bring the dog indoors so you can do your clean-up job. To clean up after your dog on the street, use a plastic bag over your hand to pick up the feces. In your yard, a "poop-scoop" is the easiest answer.

Cat feces entice many dogs, possibly because they have a different, often fishy, odor. If you have cats, look into the litter boxes that are made with narrow tunnel entrances to deter all but the most insistent of dogs. Keep the litter clean and the box in a spot that's inaccessible to your dog.

INDEX

My Sussex Spaniel

PUT YOUR PUPPY'S FIRST PICTURE HERE

Dog's Name _____

Date _____ Photographer _____